IDENTITY

defined by love

By Jenny McConnell

Publication assistance by

PAGE MASTER
PUBLISHING
PageMasterPublishing.ca

This book is dedicated to…

My husband, three beautiful boys and every Warrior Woman who is seeking love and inner peace.

It is my prayer that you will know how much you are utterly loved by your Papa God and what *He* thinks of you would define who you are more than any: achievement, job title, or recognition.

Acknowledgements

To my husband, David. Thank you for your consistent steadfast love for our family and ongoing support, strength, and loyalty through challenging times.

To Pastor Gary Meller, for your faithful dedication to Jesus and for being instrumental in my discovery of my true identity and how much I am deeply loved by my Daddy God.

To Cheryl Horn (Art Therapist) for your friendship, for teaching me how to slow down and listen, and for teaching me everything I know about art journaling.

To Warrior Women and the Round Table: Momma Rosa, Gaby, Paula, Cindy Clark (Musician and Song Writer), Sunja, and Katherine (Youth Pastor and wife to Pastor Gustavo) for your friendship, and your spiritual and emotional support.

To Pastor Rick VanDewark (C3 Edmonton Church) for your encouraging feedback.

Foreword

Too often as Christians, we can walk around with our heads down in shame, aware of our failures and brokenness, but forgetting that Jesus lives within us, making us new creations, forgiven, free and pure—giving us every reason to stand tall, victorious and confident.

McConnell's book is a series of readings and reflections that remind us of who we already are in Christ. She gently leads the reader through relevant and poignant truths from our Father, the Word, giving questions and space to guide us to deeper understandings of our inheritance and identity as loved children of God.

As a friend and sister in Christ, I've witnessed McConnell's journey of raising her own head, as she received more and more of what the Lord had for her, and from that place of a deep knowing of her Father's love, she developed a beautiful ministry to many other women. She began creating and selling compelling art pieces, each of a female—and a verse of Truth about her (our) identity—to which both believers and not-yet-believers were drawn. McConnell also began blogging about how Jesus makes Himself known to us. Concurrently, McConnell began drawing women into her home where she created an atmosphere to come together, soaking in the Lord's presence, sharing times of creative expression, intimate conversation, and prayer. McConnell was also a key figure in the forming of an online Facebook group, titled "Warrior Women—Fighting for Families," where many women share prayer requests and post words of encouragement and hope.

God has so clearly gifted McConnell in her artistic and written expression, coupled with her passion to minister to other women, so they too, would know the Father's heart for them. This book is a beautiful marriage of these talents, producing a true gift to its readers... a deeper "knowing" of who one is as a daughter of Love.

So grab your bible and your pen, and prepare to hear the Father's heart for you. Prepare to stand taller than you've ever stood. Your life will never be the same!

Written by Sherri Farbin, M.Sc

Registered Psychologist in Edmonton, AB, Canada

About the Art

I began creating these 'girls' with paraphrased scripture in 2018. Initially I submitted a couple of my 'girls' to Mosaic Magazine and the editor asked if she could put one of my 'girls' on the front cover.

A couple of months later, I picked up some copies of this magazine and headed over to an IJM (International Justice Mission) presentation about women enslaved in sex trafficking. I asked God, "what can I do?" I felt Him say, *"for every girl you sell, donate 50% of the profits to IJM."* I hadn't sold any at that stage, but since I said, "YES" to God, I have sold over 70 pieces. A month later, at the Whyte Avenue Art Walk, a lady noticed I hadn't painted any African American girls, so I painted my first one that day and declared that I would see the lady that looked like the girl I was painting. You can see a photo of her holding the painting on my 'Jenny McConnell Artist' Facebook page. Since that day, people began asking me to paint representations of loved ones as gifts. This book represents: girls and women of all nationalities.

Each girl has a heart with stitches to represent how Jesus heals our broken heart. The transparent dress, symbolises the kind of relationship Jesus wants us to have with Him. The flower represents growing in Him, and that He tends to the garden of our heart. The button represents *fastening* to Jesus in difficult times. The butterfly wing symbolises the transformation and freedom that takes place as we soak in the presence of God and enjoy a relationship with Him. The girls have a look of; vulnerability, purity, hope, and peace that we can identify with and experience when we enjoy a relationship with Jesus, the lover of our soul.

CONTENTS

How to use this book

This book explores identity and who God says we are opposed to who the world may say we are. While pain, disappointments, and hurtful people or circumstances may define us, God wants us to be defined by His love.

This book is created to explore scriptures and the truth of who we are in Jesus. Jesus said: *..you will know the truth, and the truth will set you free.* John 8:31-32

This book offers a journal portion of self reflection after each love letter that would be instrumental in leading group discussions about identity and God's promises, or to work through privately.

There are 52 devotionals, one for every week of the year, however, you can use this any time you feel like a love letter from Jesus.

Please note that these love letters hold weight because they are based on scripture and all scripture is God breathed (2 Timothy 3:16-17), however, they are still a poetic expression from my personal growth and perspective.

The scripture in this book is referenced in: English Standard Version (ESV), New International Version (NIV) and The Passion Translation (TPT).

she

is

created

in

the

image

of

LOVE

Genesis 1:27

JM 18

So God created mankind in his own image, the image of God he created them; male and female he created them.

Genesis 1:27

Dear Lovely One,

I AM Love (1 John 4:8) and I created you to be just like Me. I created you to be loved and to love just as I love you. This is your purpose and your identity. Love and Relationship.

Just as a bird was created to fly, you were created for love.

Not being loved is like clipping your wings and keeping you from flying ('The Shack' by W.P Young).

I came to give you life (John 10:10) and freedom. I came to demonstrate just how much I love you and I AM dying to have a relationship with you (John 3:16). Come to Me just as you are, nothing you have done or will do could impress Me more or make Me love you less. I just *love* you!

Forever yours,

Jesus

Reflection & Response

Welcome to your true identity in Jesus. Born to be loved and to love. What a relief to know that we are utterly and unconditionally loved just the way we are. We don't have to strive for it or earn it. It just is.

Maybe you don't believe this? Maybe like me, you have taken all the negative words and circumstances in your life and rolled them up together and created an inner dialogue that tells you, you are not enough and never will be? Of course we are all flawed in our flesh, but that is not WHO we are. WE are NOT our FLAWS. We are a CHILD of LOVE and we are LOVED. This is our identity and what defines us.

The Trinity (Father, Son, and Holy Spirit) created you and knit you together in your mother's womb (Psalm 139:13). He beholds you and sees you as altogether beautiful without flaw (Song of Songs 4:7). You are God's masterpiece (Ephesians 2:20) and *His* workmanship is marvelous (Psalm 139:13). He calls you His daughter, (Galatians 3:26) and friend (John 15:15).

You are a treasure (Exodus 19:5) and He has inscribed you on the palms of His hands (Isaiah 49:16). You are truly accepted as you are because of His Grace (1 Corinthians 15:10).

You are also valuable to Him because He has got some great work for you to do (Ephesians 2:10). He has also placed a crown on your head, which is symbolic of being part of His royal family (1 Peter 2:9) and a co-heir with Christ (Romans 8:17), seated in heavenly places with Him in His kingdom (Ephesians 2:6). Additionally, He has given you all authority over darkness (Luke 10:19).

There is so much more to your identity in Him and it will take you many years to discover it all, but this book is a good place to start.

Exercise be creative

Changing your mind to accept this new identity in Christ is a long process. It took me years before it sank into my heart and mind. The journey, however, is so worth it. So, take your time and enjoy the process.

Go back to the reflection page and write all the things God says you are. There is a lot on the internet and YouTube as well.

_____

_____

_____

_____

_____

_____

_____

_____

_____

_____

_____

_____

Write them on sticky notes and stick them around your mirror so that you can read over them each day.

she
is a
child
of
LOVE

john 1:12, 1john 3:1

Yet to all who did receive Him, to those who believed in His name, He gave the right to become children of God.

John 1:12

See what great love the Father has lavished on us, that we should be called children of God!

1 John 3:1

Dear Precious Sweet Child,

This is who you are, this is your identity. You are My child,

completely loved and adored. I delight in you and I take great pleasure in being with you. You carry many labels in this world but the only one that truly matters is that I am your Daddy God and you are My child.

Come and rest in this knowledge that you don't have to do anything to gain My love and approval. You are unconditionally loved just because you are My daughter.

I love you.

Forever yours,

Jesus

Reflection & Response

WHO WE ARE

Read John 1:9-13.

Here it indicates that the Light and the right to become His child is for everyone. He desires to be in a relationship with every one, no matter what. Sometimes people carry so much shame that they exclude themselves from this truth, but no one is exempt.

This relationship requires an acceptance and belief on our behalf and then a consistent walking and talking with Jesus to nurture that relationship.

I find the discipline of having a relationship with Jesus difficult sometimes and consistency is not my strength. I thank God that His mercies are new every morning, and if I have spent too much time away from Him, I feel the gentle pull to be quiet for a moment and say hello.

Knowing that I am His child, and that I am loved by Him unconditionally, is so important to me. I was defined by my failures and feelings of rejection for way too long. This identity caused me pain and shame, which looked like anger and rage to the people closest to me.

It wasn't until I chose to walk intimately with Jesus, that my identity, then began to shift. I am no longer defined by my weaknesses, but defined by how much my Daddy God loves me.

Exercise be creative

Write down all the positive things you like about yourself. If you can't think of anything, ask God and see what comes to mind.

_____

_____

_____

_____

_____

Write down all the thoughts, feelings, and circumstances that are weighing you down.

_____

_____

_____

_____

_____

Visualisation exercise

Imagine each thing you just wrote down weighs 5kg each. Imagine packing each of them into a backpack. How does it feel to carry all that weight around?

Now imagine putting that backpack at the feet of Jesus and saying, "I trust you with all this, please take care of it for me."

she sings a new song because LOVE has healed her heart

Psalm 147:7 & 3

He heals the broken-hearted and binds up their wounds... Sing to the Lord with grateful praise, make music to our God...

Psalm 147:3 &7

Dear Lovely One,

Come and rest in My arms of Love. I will caress and soothe your soul with My words. I will wash away your bitter disappointments. You do not need to be afraid, for I love you and even though people may abandon you, I will never leave you nor forsake you (Deuteronomy 31:6). I watch over you morning and night (Psalm 121:5-8).

I know you more intimately than anyone could and I long to hear you share your heart. I am your friend and the lover of your soul (SS 2:16). Spend time with Me in the secret place and tell Me who hurt you and how it made you feel, then forgive each person. The more you do this, the more freedom you will feel from anger and bitterness. As these feelings ebb away there will be more space left in your heart to be filled with My love. Then, when you are full, you will be able to go out and face the world again in peace. I love you.

Forever yours,

Jesus

Reflection & Response

Name the people who have caused you pain in the past and the present. Next to each of their names, write down what they said or did and how that made you feel. Ask God to help bring people to your mind.

Name: _____ what they said/ did: _____

_____

_____ how it made you feel: _____

_____

Name: _____ what they said/did: _____

_____

_____ how it made you feel: _____

_____

Name: _____ what they said/did: _____

_____

_____ how it made you feel: _____

_____

Name: _____ what they said/did: _____

_____

_____ how it made you feel: _____

_____

Group of people: _____ what they said/did: _____

_____

Exercise be creative

This could take some time and you may need to do this one exercise many times to feel the freedom from bitterness and pain.

This exercise is also useful any day a person may hurt you. Doing this has helped me to continue having a soft heart and a right spirit (Psalm 51:10).

1. In front of God, go back to the first person and imagine that they are really there in front of you.
2. Tell them what they did or said to you and tell them how it made you feel.
3. At the end of each expression of how it made you feel, say:

"I forgive you (name), I release you and I bless you."

4. Do this for every single thing that person said or did and every single hurt it made you feel.

Move onto the next person and repeat.

she is not enslaved by fear but adopted by LOVE

(Romans 8:14-15)

For those who are led by the Spirit of God are the children of God. The Spirit you received does not make you slaves, so that you live in fear again; rather the Spirit you received brought about your adoption to sonship. And by Him we call 'Abba Father.' The Spirit himself testifies with our Spirit that we are God's children. Now if we are children then we are heirs—heirs of God co-heirs with Christ.

Romans 8:14-17

Dear Chosen One,

Even though you may be forsaken by your mother or father, I will never forsake you (Psalm 27:10). I have adopted you into My kingdom, therefore you are royalty with authority (Luke 10:19). You are also unconditionally and completely loved exactly as you are (Romans 8:1).

I made you beautiful and wonderful. There is no need to feel afraid about what others might think of you. I think you are marvelous and My thoughts are all that matters. See yourself as I do. Love who I created you to be. I love you.

Forever yours,

Jesus

Reflection & Response

What was/are some positive aspects about your Mother?_____

_____

_____

What was/are some negative aspects about your Mother?_____

_____

_____

What was/are some positive aspects about your Father?_____

_____

_____

What was/are some negative aspects about your Father?_____

_____

_____

What does it mean to you personally to be adopted by God? _____

_____

_____

If God is King of Kings and Lord of Lords (1 Timothy 6:15) and if you are His child and adopted, what does that make you in His Kingdom? _____

_____

_____

Exercise be creative

Read Romans 8:14-17 again and look up, Luke 10:19, Matthew 28:18, and Matthew 17:20. What do they all have in common?

_____

_____

_____

_____

_____

What does this say about you? _____

_____

_____

_____

_____

_____

Can we earn this position or title? _____

Read: Ephesians 2:8-9. Do you consider becoming a child of God a kind of salvation? How does this new identity save us?

_____

_____

_____

_____

she

asks,

believes

and

receives

(mark 11:24)

Therefore I tell you, whatever you ask for in prayer, believe that you have received it, and it will be yours.

Mark 11:24

Dear Anointed One,

Nothing is impossible for you because of who I am in you. You can stand on my shoulders and make declarations in My Name and obstacles that are in your way will be removed (Matthew 17:20).

Know who you are in Me, believe in My Name and miracles will happen. I can only move in your life, if you persist and believe.

I love you.

Forever yours,

Jesus

Reflection & Response

Do you believe that if you ask God or make a declaration in Jesus name, that it will happen? Why or why not? _____

_____

I make declarations more than petitions now because Jesus taught me to and the bible says we have that authority in Him. I have seen a few prayers answered in this way, especially when it is coming from my heart for that person. I believe declarations from a place of love is the heart of God for all of us. When I am moved by love, I am more convinced that the declaration will come to pass.

In January 2017, it was my father in law's birthday, and we celebrated it at the local club at Minnamurra, Australia. There was a meat platter raffle and I bought a few tickets and I declared in the name of Jesus that I would win a meat platter for him. Then I asked God in my heart if He would bless Bob by letting me win. Many numbers were called out and I began to lose heart, but then all of a sudden one of my numbers came up and I was thrilled.

This week, look for opportunities to bless someone by making a declaration for them.

It could be that they are looking for a new job or someone needs a healing. Make a declaration in front of them but also go to your Papa God and ask that He would bless them.

Do not be discouraged if the declaration didn't work. Persist with a heart to want to bless others. You will see it happen, I declare it in Jesus Name. Amen.

Exercise be creative

Read James 1:6 and James 4:3, what are two factors that could prevent us receiving what we ask for? _____

_____

_____

Read Matthew 7:11 and Jeremiah 17:10. What is God saying about giving gifts and rewards?_____

_____

_____

_____

Have you ever felt powerless to change your situation?_____

Read 2 Corinthians 4:7. What does it say about God's power in us? _____

_____

_____

_____

she is called, brave and protected.

she belongs to LOVE

Isaiah 43:1

- 22 -

The Lord says, "do not fear, for I have redeemed you; I have summoned you by name; you are mine."

Isaiah 43:1

Precious Child,

You belong to Me. I will not let anything happen to you. I will be with you, even in the fire where it burns. I will hold your hand and deliver you through your pain and suffering. This affliction will not consume you (2 Corinthians 4:8).

Hang onto Me, and everything will be alright, because in Me all things are possible. I love you.

Forever yours,

Jesus

Reflection & Response

Bad things happen to good people and good things seem to happen to bad people and it's hard to understand why.

In Matthew 5:45, it mentions that our Father in Heaven causes the sun to rise on the evil and the good. It also says in Romans 2:11, that God does not show favoritism. In Romans 3:23 it says, we ALL fall short of the glory of God. In John 16:33, it says that in this world we will have trouble.

This is good news for everyone. We are all God's children and He loves us all equally. We can't earn His love or do anything to drive it away. He loves us all and blesses us all. Calamity in our lives might encourage us back into the Father's arms or refine us and go even deeper with Him. Either way, struggles and strife can be a good thing and there is hope for everyone to know the love of God in their lives.

For those who already know Jesus may experience many trials and refining to help them grow from glory to glory in Him. Maturing in Him is one of our purposes and that can hurt, but He is here to help us through it. Read: Zechariah 13:9, 1 Peter 1:6 -7, Isaiah 48:10, Proverbs 17:3.

What are you struggling with?_____

_____

_____

Do you believe God can turn your life around for good?_____

Exercise be creative

1. This week, for every struggle you have, write down each one on separate pieces of paper.

For example, I wrote 'anger' on one piece of paper, 'lack' on another, because of my finances, 'chaos' because I had so much unrest in the home. Other words might be: fear, rejection, anxiety, an illness, or disability.

2. In your kitchen sink, burn up each struggle and give it to God.

3. Find scripture that is the opposite to your struggle and make declarations like this:

"I declare that anger is no longer a part of me, I walk in peace and return a kind word." (Proverbs 15:1)

"I declare that all is going well for me and that I am content in all circumstances." (3 John 1:2, Philippians 4:11)

"I declare that I am a peacemaker and that there is peace in my home." (Matthew 5:9)

she has all her needs met by LOVE

(Philippians 4:19)

And my God will meet all your needs according to the riches of His glory in Christ Jesus.

Philippians 4:19

Dear Delightful One,

I am the everlasting God, the Alpha and Omega. The Beginning and the End, the Creator of the universe. I am also a loving Father who finds pleasure in seeing His children prosper. I delight in blessing them with good things (Matthew 7:11).

You, My sweet girl, deserve to be loved. You are worthy to have **ALL** your needs met. Come and sit with *Me*. If you spend time soaking in My presence, I will fill your cup up until it is overflowing. You do not need to go anywhere or to anyone else. Come to Me, ask Me and believe that you already have what you ask for.

The seductions of this world and the satisfaction it promises are temporary, they will only leave you parched and feeling empty. But I want to bless you with an abundant and satisfying life (John 10:10) because I love you.

Forever yours,

Jesus

Reflection & Response

Read Philippians 4:19 like this: God *WILL* supply *ALL* my needs according to *HIS RICHES* in glory in Christ Jesus.

Fill in the blanks: God _____supply _____ my needs according to _____ _____ in glory in Christ Jesus. Read it out loud three times.

This is a promise!

1. It is His *WILL* to provide—God *WILL* provide—embrace this—it is God's *WILL* to meet your needs.

2. He wants to meet *ALL* of your needs. Not some of them and not your greed. That also doesn't mean you can be wasteful. He wants you to be a good steward of what He has given you and then He will give you more (Matthew 25:23).

3. God will supply according to *HIS RICHES.* Not according to how good or perfect *you* are.

I need a loving spouse, I need to be kinder, I need to be a good steward of my income. What needs do you have? _____

_____

_____

Now ASK Him for what you need: God knows what you need before you ask (Matthew 6:32). *Ask and it SHALL be given (Matthew 7:7). All things for which you pray and ask, believe you HAVE received them (Mark 11:24).*

Believe you **HAVE** received it already and be thankful. Thanking Him is the highest form of faith. Faith doesn't say: will you? or can you? Faith says: thank you.

Exercise be creative

1. At home, make yourself and Jesus a cup of tea or coffee and place it opposite you at the dinner table.

2. Chat with Him like you would a good friend and tell Him all the things you need. Share your heart honestly with Him.

3. Thank Him for loving you, listening to you and meeting *ALL* your needs.

4. Check His cup to see if He drank from it. I've done this, but He hasn't yet.

5. Write down what changes you notice in the areas that you have asked for.

6. Persist with confidence knowing He does all things in His perfect timing.

7. Listen to what He might be asking you to do. Obedience is sometimes the key that makes changes.

———————————————————

———————————————————

———————————————————

———————————————————

———————————————————

she is
a
princess
and
belongs
to the
kingdom
of
LOVE

Galatians 4:7

You are no longer a slave but God's child; and since you are His child, God has made you also an heir.

Galatians 4:7

Sweet Child,

I am King of My Heavenly realm and you are My daughter, that makes you a princess in My Kingdom. Yes, you are royalty. You have inherited My kingdom and My Kingdom is really close to you (Matthew 3:2). That means you are able to walk in miracles like Me (John 14:12).

Just because you can't see Me and My kingdom, does not mean it is not here. They coexist simultaneously and are as close to you as your breath. Have faith to fight the good fight of freedom. Use your tongue as a double edge sword. Speak My words into existence because they will not return to me void (Isaiah 55:11).

Remember…. I love you.

Forever yours,

Jesus

Reflection & Response

I was a slave to anger for years. There was a time when I consistently declared Galatians 5:1 over myself. I paraphrased it on a piece of paper to make it personal and carried it around in my pocket. Whenever I felt angry, I would leave the house and go for a walk and read this scripture again and again. Slowly my words and behaviour turned around for good.

What do you feel enslaved by? _____

_____

Fill in the blanks: *It is for freedom that Christ has set me free from* _____
I will stand firm then, and not be burdened again by this yoke of slavery. Thank you Jesus.

Since you are a child of God, what is your royal title in God's Kingdom? _____

_____

You are royalty, therefore, you can take control of your spiritual environment and make commands and declarations. *For God has not given you a spirit of fear and timidity, but of power, love, and self discipline.* 2 Timothy 1:7

In the past, if I have felt oppressed by condemnation, I have said, "Spirit of oppression, I command you to go in Jesus' name," and I would feel it leave me.

Exercise be creative

Here are some spirits you can commanded to leave: Fear, anxiety, chaos, oppression, depression, guilt, condemnation, judgement, envy, jealousy, idolatry, manipulation, control, greed, vanity, lust, seduction, offense, rejection, addiction, anger, rage, murder, suicide, shame, self hatred, self destruction, victimisation, poverty, isolation.

Write your most common visitations.

_____

_____

_____

Take some time this week to recognise any negative feelings that begin to consume you and take charge of them.

Fill in your mission word.

"I command the spirit of _____

to get up and off me now in Jesus Name, Amen. Thank you Holy Spirit for washing me with your peace, love, and joy."

she is
a princess,
chosen and
called to
walk in
light

1 peter 2:9

But you are a chosen people, a royal priesthood, a holy nation, God's special possession, that you may declare the praises of Him who called you out of darkness into His wonderful light.

1 Peter 2:9

Dear Precious One,

I have chosen you and called you to live in My light, to bathe in My presence and walk in My glory and anointing. You are Holy and clean because of My blood that was shed for you (2 Corinthians 5:21). You do not walk in sin if you repent and choose to accept My gift of forgiveness (Acts 2:38).

I see nothing but a beautiful princess, righteous, and redeemed. You can't earn this title or position, it is a free gift given to you, should you choose to accept it. You must believe that everything, no matter how bad, is forgivable if you ask for forgiveness.

Remember I will always love you.

Forever yours,

Jesus

Reflection & Response

Do you believe that your words/actions are forgivable?_____

Read this promise:

*If we **confess** our sins, He is faithful and just and **will forgive** us our sins and **purify us** from all unrighteousness.* (1 John 1:9)

What do we need to do first before we are forgiven? _____

What will Father God do if we confess? _____

Read Matthew 18:22. How often do we need to confess our sins? _____

_____

*In Him we have redemption through His blood, the forgiveness of sins, in accordance with the riches of God's Grace. (*Ephesians 1:7)

This scripture is talking about how Jesus died on the cross for our sins once and for all. We are forgiven, He was the final atonement, He tore the veil of shame that kept us from having a relationship with Papa God. Now, because of Jesus, Father God does not see our sin, our mess, and we receive the gift of eternal life. However, according to 1 John 1:9 we need to confess our sins to Papa God every time we do wrong.

Why do they seem to conflict?

Ephesians 1:7 is talking about salvation for now *and* forever and the atonement of our sin, so we can enjoy the privilege of entering into a relationship with our Father. Salvation for us *means* being *with* Him, now and for all eternity. Like all relationships though, they need to be maintained with loyalty and faithfulness. When we go against what Father God wants, we are breaking our relationship with Him.

We are saved by His Grace and not by anything we do and He will always love us and be there for us, however to maintain that relationship, that salvation, we do need to ask for forgiveness every time we sin against Him and Holy Spirit will gently let us know when we need to.

Exercise be creative

This week, read these sentences out loud every day:

1. I am chosen by my Papa God.

2. I am holy and clean.

3. I am royalty.

4. I am called to walk with Him.

If you do or say something you feel in your heart is going against what your Father God wants, ask Him for forgiveness immediately and believe you are forgiven.

If you begin to dwell on your mistakes, command the spirit of condemnation to get up and off you in Jesus Name.

Extra Notes

_____

_____

_____

_____

_____

_____

_____

_____

she
is
called,
brave and
protected
she belongs
to
LOVE

(Isaiah 43:1)

But now, this is what the Lord says—He who created you, Jacob, He who formed you, Israel; "Do not fear, for I have redeemed you; I have summoned you by name, you are mine."

Isaiah 43:1

Dear Courageous One,

I am with you wherever you go. I will not let anything harm you. Even if it hurts and you feel the pressure coming in from all sides, I am here holding you through the affliction. Your trust in Me will make you brave.

Dear little one, don't give up now, nothing can overtake you because you are Mine! I won't let the enemy win. Rest assured, in the end he loses and you will reap the victory if you remain in Me.

I love you.

Forever yours,

Jesus

Reflection & Response

Your parents, siblings, and spouse may know you pretty well, but they don't know *everything* about you. God, however, knows you fully. He knows what you are thinking and feeling every day.

Are you going through something now that no one could possibly understand?

What does it mean to you when God says, *"you are Mine?"*_____

_____

_____

Before I formed you in the womb I knew you, before you were born, I set you apart. (Jeremiah 1:5) This was not just for Jeremiah, this is for all of us. What does this mean for you?_____

_____

_____

For you created my inmost being; you knit me together in my mother's womb. (Psalm 139:13). What does inmost being mean to you? _____

_____

_____

My husband and I talk about loving each other's who-ness. When you strip away all the: rejection, offense, hurts, disappointments, anxiety, pride, and stress, your who-ness comes out, the person God created you to be. That's why He wants you to trust Him completely with everything, so you can be left with who He created you to be and live in peace and joy.

Exercise be creative

Write down all the labels you have been wearing, that do not benefit you.

_____

_____

_____

_____

Now, read your list as if you are a parent of that child. Visualise removing each label and write the labels you would want that child to have instead.

_____

_____

_____

_____

Read this every day for a week.

You are altogether beautiful, my darling; there is no flaw in you.

(Song of Solomon 4:7)

she

is   only

driven

by

LOVE

philippians 2:3-4

Do nothing out of selfish ambition or vain conceit. Rather, in humility value others above yourselves, not looking at your own interests but each of you to the interests of others.

Philippians 2:3-4

Sweet Child of Mine,

I have called you and redeemed you to Myself. I know your inner thoughts and secrets and I love you. My love for you is enough. You do not need to find value or worth in the approval of others, nor do you need to compete with anyone else, this will only exhaust you.

But I have come to give you: love, life, and rest. I want you to know deep down that there is nothing you can do to make Me love you more (Romans 8:38-39). When you truly believe this, you will experience a freedom to love others as I love you, and put their needs first the same way I died for you.

Forever yours,

Jesus

Reflection & Response

What competitive sports did you play as a child?_____

What other areas of your life were you encouraged to compete in?_____

_____

_____

How did you feel when you lost or others were better than you?_____

_____

Is it easy to be happy for others when they succeed?_____

As a child, were you exposed to encouragement or condemnation when you failed?

_____

We live in a competitive world, and we are taught that it's good to have healthy competition. If it is not stewarded properly, however, it can become twisted in our thinking that if someone is better than us at something, then we somehow don't measure up, that we are not good enough. The more experiences we have of not being or feeling good enough, the more our inner dialogue becomes, "I am not enough" or "I am a failure" and this brings shame, which can result in us having, low self worth, feeling angry, and feeling like a victim.

From this painful perspective of low self esteem it might be easy to see others as better, but only at the cost of feeling worse ourselves and can result in us feeling jealous or envious. It is then impossible for us to esteem others higher than ourselves in a healthy way.

Learning to love myself exactly as I am has taken years. Reading the truth about myself from God's perspective has significantly healed my heart and changed my inner dialogue, and for the first time ever, I can truly be happy for other people's success because I know how much My God loves *me*, that He has a hope and a future for *me* and that He is working in and through *me* for *my* good.

Exercise be creative

God's greatest commandment is to love Him with everything we have and love others (Matthew 22:37). LOVE is our purpose.

But it says in 1 John 4:19 that we love, because He *first* loved us.

In order to even love God and then others, we need to know how much we are loved.

This week spend some time with Father God and ask Him to show you personally how much He loves you.

Take a courageous step and be specific.

For example and to cut the story short, I asked God for a bangle if He thought I was a good mom. I asked if He would give it to me the following day or I would forget that I even asked. The very next day my girlfriend, Katherine, gave me a bangle and said, "Holy Spirit told me to give you this."

Write down how you want God to show you that He loves you. Ask Him from your heart, later write the results.

_____

_____

_____

_____

she is
strengthened
and
empowered
by
LOVE

isaiah 40:29

JM'19

He gives strength to the weary and increases the power of the weak.

Isaiah 40:29

Dearest Child,

At times you feel you can't go on. Sometimes it is so hard for so long that you can't see an end to all the chaos and disappointment. I understand. I feel everything you feel. I cry with you and I want to tell you everything will be all right.

Come away with Me (Song of Songs 2:10), draw your strength from Me. Spend time with Me and pour your heart out. Ask for what you need and I will give it to you. I love you so much and I desire to give you good things. All you need to do is sit with Me and ask.

Forever yours,

Jesus

Reflection & Response

Come to Me all who are weary and burdened, and I will give you rest. Take My yoke upon you and learn from Me, for I am gentle and humble in heart, and you will find rest for your souls. For My yoke is easy and My burden is light. (Matthew 11:28-30)

Both verses talk about going to Jesus, spending time with Him, laying it all down and letting go. He promises us rest and strength if we go to Him and trust Him.

Trusting Jesus has been one of the hardest things I have had to learn to do because I love to be in control of the outcomes. So often I try to do things my way in my own strength, which only ends up frustrating and exhausting me and preventing God from doing it the right way in His perfect timing.

What is His yoke? Yoke indicates some work which seems contradictory to resting in Him, however, if we read John 6:29 it says, *This is the work of God, that you believe in Him whom He has sent.* If we read John 15:4 it says*, remain in Me.* So this is our yoke or work, to believe or trust Him and to obey/abide/remain in Him.

What burdens are you carrying right now?_____

_____

_____

Sometimes I need to repeat scripture over and over again before I can actually do it. This is one of my favorites: *Trust the Lord with all your heart and lean not on your own understanding but in all your ways acknowledge Him and He will make your paths straight.* (Proverbs 3:5)

Exercise be creative

This week take some time each day and just sit with Jesus. You don't have to say anything, just visualize that He is really there. Allow Him to listen to your heart or groaning (Romans 8:26). Feel His presence. Give Him 10-15 minutes.

Describe what you felt.

_____

_____

_____

_____

_____

Write down what you need and trust Him with your list.

_____

_____

_____

_____

_____

she

waits with

expectation

Psalm 5:3

In the morning, Lord, you hear my voice, in the morning I lay my

requests before you and wait expectantly.

Psalm 5:3

Oh Captivating One,

I love listening to you. Please come and talk to Me and share with Me your hearts' desires. I hear your prayers and I delight in working for your good. Come to Me with an expectant heart and do not become impatient or lose faith when circumstances don't bend within your timing.

There is a reason why I ask you to wait, sometimes it's for your refining and growth. Always remember that I can do immeasurably more than all you ask or imagine (Ephesians 3:20), so keep your eyes open for unexpectant outcomes and don't let go, I am showing you something.

Never forget, I love you.

Jesus

Reflection & Response

What strikes you the most about Psalm 5:3? _____

_____

_____

One of the most difficult things I have found in my relationship with God is the waiting for promises fulfilled. I am not a patient person and I am still waiting for prayers to be answered that I have been praying into consistently for 8 years and longer.

Proverbs 13:12 says, *Hope deferred makes the heart sick, but a longing fulfilled is a tree of life*. When I think of a tree of life, I also think of the fruit of the Spirit because fruit is grown on trees. I remember asking God for the fruit of the Spirit years ago in earnest (Galatians 5:22) because I didn't want to be an angry mom anymore, I wanted: love, joy, peace, patience, etc. Since then I realise, He doesn't just make you patient, He puts you through circumstances that will test your patience until you have mastered it. Practice really does make perfect.

It is God's desire that we keep growing to be like Him (2 Corinthians 3:18), because as we do, we become a tree of life for others. The more we spend time with God and meditate on His words, the more we are like a tree planted in living waters that yields good fruit and leaves for healing (Psalm 1:3 & Revelation 22:2).

So just maybe the longer we wait, the more of a life giving tree we become for others and the fulfillment becomes a testimony that encourages others to keep going.

Exercise be creative

What have you been hoping or praying for? _____

_____

_____

_____

What do you think God might be teaching you while you wait? _____

_____

_____

_____

_____

Have you been encouraged by someone else's testimony? _____

The Spirit of Prophecy who bears testimony to Jesus. Revelation 19:10

In other words, someone else's testimony or Jesus journey, can be a prophetic word or a future story for my own life too.

Someone else's story encourages my faith and gives me the strength to keep going.

she
experiences
beyond
her
understanding
the deep
fullness of
LOVE

(Ephesians 3:19)

I pray that you...may have power to grasp how wide and long and high and deep is the LOVE of Christ, and to know this love that surpasses knowledge—that you may be filled to the measure of all fullness of God.

Ephesians 3:17-19

My Daughter,

I long to fill you up with My love, to tell you hidden secrets and to pour Myself out on you. I long to have a relationship with you! But relationships grow with time. Like anything that is good for you, it requires discipline to experience this kind of relationship with Me.

Talk to Me, I'm listening. Listen to Me, I'm speaking to you through the Scriptures and to your spirit in every day circumstances. Open your heart, your eyes, and your ears. Ask Me to help you do this every day.

We are about to embark on a beautiful journey together. Stay on course! It will be well worth the ride.

No matter what though, I love you.

Forever yours,

Jesus

Reflection & Response

Are you ready to go deeper with God?_____Are you prepared to do whatever it takes to experience the fullness of what God has for you?_____

It is time then to put God first in your life and trust Him completely.

Write down all the things and people you give priority to in your life _____

_____

_____

God has called me to love Him with all my heart, mind and soul (Luke 10:27), but I can often jump back and forth between putting God first or making: my husband, sex, fun, money, movies, chocolate, or my ministry an idol. All these idols gratify the flesh and often lead to; dissatisfaction, restlessness, destruction, and I end up suffering. God however, asks me to rise above these things with Him and walk in the Spirit which leads to life, peace, and joy. In this place I experience the *love* and *fullness* He has for me. He has also taught me the POWER of fasting food to help me get there.

Reflect on these words:

You shall have no other gods before Me - Exodus 20:3

Walk by the Spirit, and you will not gratify the desires of the flesh – Galatians 5:16

Those who cling to worthless idols turn away from God's love for them – Jonah 2:8

Those who run after gods will suffer more and more – Psalm 16:4

Put to death...whatever belongs to your earthly nature: sexual immorality, lust, evil desires and greed, which is idolatry – Colossians 3:5

So we fasted and implored our God... He listened... – Ezra 8:23

But this kind of demon is cast out only through prayer and fasting - Matthew 17:21 – TPT

Exercise be creative

Jesus talked about fasting as being a re-quirement. The most incredible miracles I ever experienced, was when I fasted.

Jesus said in Matthew 6:16: and *when* you fast, not *if* you fast.

Read: Isaiah 58:3-7, Joel 2:12, Daniel 10:3

1. This week choose to fast something every day that would be hard for you. It doesn't have to be food.

2. Choose to get up 5-10 minutes earlier and read a chapter of your bible and ask God to come and fill you up with all His fullness. Ask for what you need.

3. At the end of the day before bed, read another chapter of your bible and thank Him for all He is doing.

As you do this every day, you might start to see and hear God speak to you. How is God talking to you this week?

_____

_____

_____

_____

_____

she

is filled

with hope,

joy and

peace

as she

trusts

in

LOVE

Romans 15:13

May the God of hope fill you with all joy and peace as you trust in Him,

so that you may overflow with hope by the power of the Holy Spirit.

Romans 15:13

My Sweet Love,

Letting go and completely trusting Me is the hardest thing for you to do. The temptation is to work life out on your own or to fix your own problems. But I have the power to change people and circumstances far more than you do. All you need to do is ask Me, wait and hope.

The reward for letting go and trusting Me is Joy and Peace. This fruit will become yours as you continue to enjoy a relationship with Me and trust Me. I love you.

Forever yours,

Jesus

Reflection & Response

TRUST is the key to PEACE and JOY.

What areas in your life do you have a hard time letting go of?_____

_____

_____

For me, it was: my husband's smoking, his walk with Jesus, and inability to love me in ways I wanted to be loved. I wanted to change all these areas and I couldn't. I only drove him away more and made us both miserable. Letting go of my husband and his choices has been and sometimes still is, my biggest challenge.

God, however, has been teaching me to come to Him with my heart and tell Him everything. I often sob in His presence as I unload my hurting heart and my fears. Letting go of every area of my life - husband, kids, and finances and completely trusting in God to take care of everyone and everything is so liberating and I some-times get a good taste of what it feels like to live like a child without a worry or a concern. When I am in that place of complete surrender, life is so easy, I feel the peace and child-like joy even if my circumstances still seem bleak.

Write down all your hurts and concerns._____

_____

_____

_____

Exercise be creative

1. Write down on separate pieces of paper every concern you have.

2. Find a box (jewellery box?) to put them into.

3. Say: I release __(say concern)__ to you Jesus and trust that you will take care of it/him/her.

4. As you say each one, place it in the box.

5. In the week, if you feel a specific concern creep back into your mind, say number 3 again.

6. Don't try and do anything about your concerns, just put it back in the box and give it to Jesus.

How has this exercise helped you?

_____

_____

_____

_____

_____

_____

_____

_____

she finds shelter under the wings of LOVE

Psalm 91:4

He will cover you with His feathers, and under His wings you will find

refuge; His faithfulness will be your shield and rampart.

Psalm 91:4

Beautiful One,

The enemy is prowling around looking for someone to devour (1 Peter 5:8). I have defeated death on the cross, that victory is won but attacks from the enemy will still rise up against you until I come back. However, I will fight for you (Exodus 14:14), if you ask Me. When you have no more energy left, tell Me and then rest and trust in Me.

Call out to Me and I will send angels to stand guard and fight for you also and ask Holy Spirit to minster to your mind. Take captive of every thought (2 Corinthians 10:5). Do not listen to the lies of the enemy. You are My daughter and you have authority over darkness (Luke 10:19).

I will never leave you because I love you.

Forever yours,

Jesus

Reflection & Response

When you feel under attack, there are three responses: Fight, Flight, and Freeze. What is your most common response?_____

My response is *fight* every time. This has not served me well in the natural, but very well in the supernatural. What Satan means for evil, God can turn around for good (Romans 12:21, 2 Corinthians 12:9). Of course, this is a process. It is very hard to work against our natural instincts, which is why walking by the Spirit daily is so important.

The enemy is relentless, he knows human nature well and the trappings that trip them up. We have authority to tell him to shut up and get out, in the Name of Jesus. If I start to feel worried, scared, or oppressed, I'll tell that spirit to get up and off me in the name of Jesus.

Sometimes though, the battle is heavy and too many things are happening at once. I might feel overwhelmed and exhausted. This is the time I cry out to Jesus to fight for me.

This is the time I curl up in His lap and ask Him to send His angels to fight for Me. We have an army of angels that bring Glory to God and are assigned to each one of us and we can ask Papa God to send us our angels to fight for us.

Exercise be creative

Read: Exodus 23:20, Psalm 91:11,
Matthew 18:10, Hebrews 1:14.

What do they all have in common?

_____

_____

_____

_____

_____

If you are feeling overwhelmed, pray this:

Father God, thank you for the angels that you have assigned to me. I ask that you send them now to fight for me. I ask they will guard and protect me in Jesus Name.

If your body is under attack, pray this:
Father God I ask that you will send angels to minister to my body and I thank you for healing it, in Jesus name.

If your mind feels under attack, pray this:
Holy Spirit I ask that you minister to my mind. I take captive of every thought and make it obedient to the mind of Christ.
(2 Corinthians 10:5).

she
is
free
because
of
TRUTH

(john 8:36)

So if the Son sets you free, you will be free indeed.

John 8:36

Lovely One,

I have called you to Myself. I am your Father, Brother, Husband, and Lover of your soul. I have set you free from the limitations of your mind and the seductions of this world. You are no longer a slave but a member of My family (Romans 8:15-17).

You are no longer alone or abandoned but adopted into My Kingdom. Read the Word for I am the Word (John 1:1) and abide in Me (1 John 2:6) and you will experience true freedom. I love you.

Forever yours,

Jesus

Reflection & Response

Write down the ways in which you feel trapped. _____

_____

_____

_____

I felt very trapped by my anger and the intensity of my emotions. I carried so much shame from a lifetime of academic failure connected with my learning disabilities that I wasn't even aware of. Choosing to go deep with Jesus was the best decision of my life. Over the years He slowly peeled the layers away and revealed to me all kinds of things I needed to know. The most important one is how much I am utterly loved just the way I am. I was set free from self hatred, condemnation, and shame. Over time I learned to love and accept myself, just the way I am.

Jesus didn't just save me from sin and death (Romans 6:23, 1 John 3:5) and He didn't just come to give me eternal life. He also came to save me from my own destructive self and give me a new and wonderful life (2 Corinthians 5:17, Psalm 25:5) with new purpose that brings me peace and joy (Jeremiah 29:11, Ephesians 2:10).

Jesus also came to set us free from sickness and disease (1 Peter 2:24, Jeremiah 17:14), heart ache (Psalm 147:3), and condemnation (Isaiah 54:4, Romans 8:1, Hebrews 12:2).

He truly wants to bless us and set us free.

Exercise be creative

Sometimes when we feel trapped we need to listen to the voice of God and ask Him what is it He wants us to do to experience freedom.

This week pick one thing that you feel you need to be set free from.

Spend some time with God and ask Him what does He want you to do. A thought might come to mind, trust that it is God speaking and write it down here.

_____

_____

Ask God for confirmation of that thought. Pick up the bible and randomly go to any page, or download a devotional app, and read the word for the day. Sometimes God speaks directly to my situation in these ways. Be patient and keep your ears and eyes open. He will speak to you in a unique way and when He does, obey.

_____

_____

_____

she has TRUTH and is free from condemnation

Romans 8:1

Therefore, there is now no condemnation in Christ Jesus, because through Christ Jesus the law of the Spirit, who gives life, has set you free from the law of sin and death.

Romans 8:1-2

My Precious Love,

When I look at you, My bride, all I see is beauty, a lovely garden of woven complexity. I died to set you free from all guilt and condemnation. You are a clean, blank canvas. Every day My mercies are new (Lamentations 3:22-23). You don't need to hide from Me for I love every part of you. Yes, I love your mess too!

Come to Me and tell Me everything, I will never reject you. Ask for My forgiveness and I will always give it to you. If you need to be forgiven every day, then ask and you will receive it every day (Matthew 18:21-22). I paid the price for all your sins and it is finished (John 19:28-30).

So walk in confidence knowing that I see you altogether beautiful without flaw (Song of Solomon 4:7). Accept My love into your life and you will never need to feel alone again. Discard what others might think and only care what I think... because, I love you.

Forever yours,

Jesus

Reflection & Response

What is the one thing that you constantly feel guilty about?_____

_____

I always felt guilty about yelling at, or smacking my children. I would berate myself every time. I knew that responding in patience and kindness rather than reacting was how I was meant to bring them up, but it seemed impossible to break the anger cycle.

In Romans 7:15-19 it says: *I'm a mystery to myself, for I want to do what is right, but I end up doing what my moral instincts condemn. And if my behaviour is not in line with my desire, my conscience still confirms the excellence of the law. And now I realise it is no longer my true self doing it, but the unwelcome intruder of sin in my humanity. For I know that nothing good lives within the flesh of my fallen humanity. The longings to do what is right are within me, but willpower is not enough to accomplish it. My lofty desires to do what is good are dashed when I do the things I want to avoid. So, if my behaviour contradicts my desires to do good, I must conclude that it's not my true identity doing it, but the unwelcome intruder of sin hindering me from being who I really am.* The Passion Translation.

I love the way The Passion Translation interprets this struggle that Paul was feeling. It was exactly how I felt for years. It's very easy to condemn ourselves. Equally, it's also easy to quickly judge others or be judged. I sometimes felt alone at church, being amongst Christians who seemed to have it all together. I felt sick amongst the healthy (Mark 2:17).

Other times, moms I didn't even know would walk right up to me and tell me exactly what they thought of my boy's behaviour and how I should handle them. Life and people can be stressful and it can make you want to run away and isolate yourself. Jesus, however, never judges or condemns us and He always invites us to sit with Him and pour out our hearts.

Exercise be creative

Change is possible, but it takes time, patience, and grace. God has these things in abundance, so don't give up.

1. Every morning ask: *"Lord, create in me a clean heart and renew a right spirit in me today."* (Psalm 51:10)

2. Offer the things up to God you are struggling with. *"Father, today I ask that you would help me with* _____

   _____
   _____*."*

3. Before bed, if you slipped up, say: *"Father forgive me for* _____

   _____
   _____*."*

4. Do this every time you need to. His mercies are new every morning and He will forgive you every time you ask.

5. Remember you are forgiven immediately, so forgive yourself.

6. If any voice, including your own, gives you a hard time say: *"There is no condemnation in Christ Jesus, I will get there... eventually."*

7. Remember, we *all* sin and fall short of the glory of God (Romans 3:23), no exceptions.

she
speaks
healing
words,
sweet
like
honey

Proverbs 16:24

Gracious words are honeycomb, sweet to the soul and healing to the bones.

Proverbs 16:26

Dear Sweet Child,

Sometimes you have a hard time speaking words of life over yourself and others. The human heart is fragile and toxic words cut deep. You believe the hurtful words spoken over you and from that belief your identity is formed and from *that* place you speak hurtfully and so the cycle continues.

Spend time with Me and read *My* words. Come to know how much I adore you and made you perfect just the way you are.

I hold your face in My hands and say: "Daughter I made you like this and you are beautiful!"

The more you read what I think about you, the more you will believe it and not the lies you think about yourself. Only then will you be able to speak love and life over others. You can't change yourself easily, but with Me all things are possible (Matthew 19:26).

And remember, no matter what, I love you.

Forever yours,

Jesus

Reflection & Response

Sometimes while growing up, parents, siblings, teachers, and friends can say hurtful things that cut deep. Even when humour is used it can be incredibly hurtful. Have you been hurt by the words people have spoken over you and your life? What words were these? _____

_____

_____

_____

_____

During my upbringing, I felt like a failure and a constant disappointment. Discouraging words were frequently spoken over me. These words began to define me, and it shaped how I spoke to others as well.

When I started having a family of my own, Jesus highlighted my thought and word life. In 2014, I ran away with Jesus. I got up early and spent an hour with Him each morning. For just over a year, I prayed, worshiped, and read my bible and devotional books (Heidi & Roland Baker, Sarah Young and Joyce Meyer). His words began to undo the belief system I had about myself. I was literally having my brain washed clean of all the muck and having it replaced with His truth.

Did you know we can be brainwashed to believe certain things about ourselves? It's time to start knowing and believing what Papa God thinks of us.

Exercise be creative

Read Chapter 2 of Song of Solomon. It is also an allegory of the feelings Jesus has for us. Write all the words that fill you up with His love.

_____

_____

_____

_____

_____

_____

_____

_____

_____

_____

_____

_____

_____

_____

_____

_____

_____

_____

_____

she has

hope

and

waits

for

LOVE

Psalm 130:5

- 78 -

I wait for the Lord, my whole being waits, and in His word I put my hope.

Psalm 130:5

Wait for the Lord; be strong, and let your heart take courage; wait for the Lord!

Psalm 27:14

My Sweet Love,

Sometimes when you pray you expect to see results immediately. I work in that way sometimes, but more often than not, I am in the process of working all things for your good (Romans 8:28) and that can feel like a lifetime to you (Psalm 90:4).

Take heart, be patient, keep your eyes on Me and do not be distracted by your circumstances. Keep sharing your heart with Me and trust Me. I am not just working in your circumstances, I am working in you, because I love you.

Forever yours,

Jesus

Reflection & Response

What are you hoping for? What do you want to see change in your life?

_____

_____

_____

Sometimes we feel 'Trapped in Transition' (Elevation Church Sermon), we are waiting for change and sometimes we have been asking and waiting for many years. Transition is difficult, it is unsettling and uncomfortable, but if we rush ahead and make rash decisions we can miss the miracle, we can miss the transformation in our transition.

You have often heard the saying, it is the journey and not the destination. It is a cliché that rings true.

I once had a dream that I went through the back door of a house. I was taking a short cut to get to the other side. In my dream, I noticed that the house was empty of all the furniture. Half way through, I noticed a man painting the floors with gloss, he stopped and looked up at me in shock. I looked down and noticed that my feet were bare and that the floor was still wet and sticky. When I looked back, I could see that I had ruined the floors and that I was stuck. I couldn't move forward to get to my destination or I would ruin everything.

This was a huge lesson for me. Jesus was telling me there are no shortcuts to long lasting and worthwhile miracles and change. Transformation takes time, and I must not hurry the process, but take the long way around with Him.

Exercise be creative

What lessons is Jesus trying to show you during your time of transition? If you are not sure, ask Him, "Jesus what do you want to teach me in this time?" Write down what He is showing you this week.

_____

_____

_____

_____

_____

_____

_____

_____

_____

_____

_____

_____

_____

_____

_____

_____

_____

she
is
healed
and
crowned
with
LOVE
and
compassion

psalm 103:3,4

Praise the Lord...who forgives all your sins and heals all your diseases, who redeems your life from the pit and crowns you with love and compassion, who satisfies your desires with good things...

Psalm 103: 2-5

My Dearest Friend,

Forgiveness is the key to healing your heart and body. If you are hurting, you may need to forgive someone. Forgive what they did, forgive how it made you feel, forgive many times over until you feel a release from that person.

I came to give you an abundant life (John 10:10); I came also to free you from all guilt of sin because you are completely forgiven for every wrong choice you have ever made or ever will make. If you feel convicted, just ask for forgiveness. I have clothed you with righteousness (2 Corinthians 5:21). You are clean and pure in My Father's eyes because of My sacrifice on the cross. Please know I died for you, because I love you.

Ask for what your heart desires and trust that I want to give you good things. Be patient and keep asking, even if it takes years. Remember that I make all things beautiful and My timing is perfect (Ecclesiastes 3:11)

I take My time because you are worth it, and because I love you.

Forever yours,

Jesus

Reflection & Response

Forgiveness is the key to being healed not only in your heart but in your body also.

Back in 2015, Jesus taught me the power of forgiveness when I went to my prayer group at Terwillegar Community Church. I remember my friend, Cheryl Horn, asking me to pray for her friend who had chronic stomach cramps and came to ask for prayer.

As I knelt at her feet, I felt an enormous pressure around the back of my head. I was commanding the pain and affliction to leave in the name of Jesus, but this pressure got so intense I couldn't ignore it anymore. I asked if she had any pain at the back of her head. She didn't, but because she was studying to be a counsellor, she was able to inform me that, that area of the brain was responsible for emotions. Since I had just read the book: 'Essential Guide to Healing' by Randy Clark and Bill Johnson, I was able to discern that her stomach cramps were related to the need to forgive someone or many people.

I asked her if she had people in her life that she needed to forgive, and she did. I asked her to say out loud that she forgives each person that had hurt her. This was hard for her to do at first, but as she did and when she finished, her pain and the pain at the back of my head left.

We cannot underestimate the power of forgiveness. It is what Jesus did. He forgave, healed, and delivered. He set people free and that is still His heart for everyone today.

Exercise be creative

Sometimes I need to forgive people daily.

This is how I keep my heart from becoming hard and bitter.

Write down the people that hurt you frequently. _____

_____

_____

Imagine they are right in front of you and say,

"I forgive you (name) for (what they did/said) your actions/words made me feel (insignificant, rejected, unworthy, shame, etc.) But in the presence of God, I forgive you, in Jesus Name."

Sometimes you may need to bring these people before the Lord in your quiet time many times until your heart catches up with your words. Like anything, this could be a long process.

she delights in LOVE and is given the desires of her heart

Psalm 37:4

Take delight in the Lord, and He will give you the desires of your heart. Commit your way to the Lord; trust Him and He will do this...Be still before the Lord and wait patiently for Him...

(Psalm 37:4-5,7)

Precious Child,

Like any doting Father, I love to give good things to My children, and like any good Father, I long to have a relationship with you. Spend time with Me, I treasure your company. Sing to Me, I love to hear your voice. Share your heart with Me, I love to listen to you. Seek Me and learn to hear My voice, I long to tell you secret mysteries you do not know (Jeremiah 33:3). Read about Me and My character and what I think of you, you may be surprised to learn how much I adore and value you. I am not the angry God that others paint Me out to be.

When we become close like this, you will begin to ask from Me with right motives (James 4:3). Your Spirit will resonate with Mine and we will work together as one. Then I will open the flood gates of My Glory upon you and you will see miracles happen. I love you.

Forever yours,

Jesus

Reflection & Response

There is one thing I have learned in my walk with Jesus. He loves to bless us and demonstrate His love for us, but not in ways we sometimes want. God has worked more powerfully through me when my heart and desire is to see others blessed.

Summer 2019, I took my boys camping to Elk island. My boys have been there a few times before, but have never seen a Bison up close, even on the Bison loop. So I declared out loud in the name of Jesus that we would see a Bison. Just 3 seconds later, there was a massive Bison grazing by the side of the road closest to me. We, of course, were so excited and stopped and took lots of photos. Then we kept driving and a few seconds later we saw another Bison, sitting on the side of the road closest to my son. He was so excited and exclaimed: "Mom, I just prayed quietly to myself that we would see another Bison!" We all felt so blessed and it was a moment of recognising how much Jesus hears our prayers and loves us. We never did see another Bison for the rest of our camping trip, which in fact made the time we did, that much more special.

God has a purpose for each one of us to honour and serve Him and to bring the Kingdom of Heaven to others. He has not called us to our own comfort, but for His own good pleasure. He desires a relationship with us and when we take that relationship seriously and become close to Him, we adopt His heart for others. We also walk in the knowledge and purpose of who He is and sometimes, miracles happen. However sometimes, we are just waiting for a breakthrough in our marriage, family, health, or finances and no matter how much we pray and declare, things don't seem to shift. That is when we need to completely trust Him for His perfect timing and know that letting go and keeping our eyes fixed on Him and not our circumstances is the only way forward. Sudden changes are the miracles we hope for but often we are not ready for them until we have walked through the process of transformation.

Exercise be creative

What desires of your heart are you wanting to bring before the Lord today?

_____

_____

_____

_____

Sit quietly before your Papa God and bring one of your desires before Him. Ask Him what does He think. Read some Scripture and with a devotion write down what He might be telling you. Ensure you obey.

_____

_____

_____

_____

_____

_____

_____

_____

_____

Do this with all your desires.

she
hangs onto
LOVE,
her
refuge
in
times
of
trouble

Psalm 9:9

The Lord is a refuge for the oppressed, a stronghold in times of trouble. Those who know your name trust in you, for you Lord, have never forsaken those who seek you.

Psalm 9:9-10

My Dear Queen,

When the storm rages around you, come to Me. I long to wrap my arms of comfort around you and tell you that everything will be okay. I love you so passionately in ways that no one else ever could. I AM Love and Peace and when you rest *in* Me you will experience all that I AM.

When you come and share your heart with Me, you are giving Me the opportunity to fill you up with Myself. This time with Me will strengthen you to face a day of potential disappointments and temptations.

Know that you are never alone. I am always here waiting for you because I love you.

Forever yours,

Jesus

Reflection & Response

Do you ever go through moments where you just feel overwhelmed, oppressed, or sad and you're not even sure why? It could be a physical, hormonal, mental, or spiritual issue and sometimes it's hard to even know what to pray. If I am ever unsure, I go straight to spiritual first and command the spirit of oppression to go in the name of Jesus. It is quick and easy and is often all I need to do in that moment. If the feelings persist, and especially over time, I would ask Jesus to help me find the root and together we may go on a journey.

Sometimes we are battling against years of exposure to obstacles, hardships, or trauma as a child. Deliverance can be ongoing and it can be psychological and spiritual. Seeing a psychologist as well as people qualified and experienced at doing deliverances can be extremely healing. I have been to 'Desert Streams' many times; they are an incredible ministry. Lots of Pentecostal churches have healing rooms and are able to do similar things. Ask Jesus where you need healing and where you should go to get the support.

Sometimes our battle is for loved ones. Jesus wants us to lay it all at His feet and trust Him. Having a support prayer partner or team of prayer warriors around you is also an enormous benefit, *for where two or three gather in my name, there am I with them.* Matthew 18:20 Above all else, spend time each day with Jesus, pour out your heart and concerns and then wait and rest in Him.

Exercise be creative

Are you facing some incredibly difficult situations right now? What are they?

_____

_____

_____

_____

_____

Every morning or evening, offer your list up to God and ask Him to take care of it for you.

Say: "Father God, I keep my eyes on you and I release every concern I have into your hands. I ask that you will take care of (read above list) and I let go and trust you with all these things. Thank you for loving me and never letting me go. Help me to rest in you and know that you will take care of everything and everyone in your perfect timing. In Jesus Name, Amen."

she is
hidden in
TRUTH
and sets
her
mind
on
things
above

(Colossians 3:2-3)

Set your mind on things above, not on earthly things. For you died, and your life is now hidden with Christ in God.

Colossians 3:2-3

Dearest One,

When you take captive of every thought that oppresses you and meditate on My words, you will experience My perspective that will lighten you.

Keeping your mind on Me (Colossians 3:2) will also help you rise above the seduction of deceptive pleasures and false joy. The world chases after these things, but they are often left feeling empty and alone.

The struggle for you will always be between your spirit and flesh. Your spirit cries out for more of Me but your flesh wants to be indulged. I say to you today, don't give into the flesh but come away with Me often and live by the Spirit (Galatians 5:16-18).

My desire is that you experience a sweet life filled with hope, peace and joy because I love you.

Forever yours,

Jesus

Reflection & Response

I have been crucified with Christ, it is no longer I who live but Christ who lives in me.
Galatians 2:20 What does this mean to die or to no longer live?

_____

_____

In 2014, I was struggling so much with being a mom and a wife that I felt ready to throw the towel in and run away. That is when the above Scripture came to my mind, and that is when I set up my 'war room' in a storage room and got up every morning for one hour for just over a year. It put my whole walk with Jesus back on track in ways I have never experienced before.

My journey began and still remains with this one theme: ***Dying to Self.***

I recognize how selfish and self- centered I can be, how easily affected I am by people and circumstances. I also recognize how easily I can play the victim or give in to my emotions. Jesus calls me higher, to put away my own wants and desires and to chase after His heart desiring to: think like Him, perceive like Him, walk like Him, and be hidden *in* Him.

Jesus taught me how fasting is a helpful and practical strategy for putting the flesh to death and living by the Spirit (Romans 8:5-17). It was the hardest thing for me to do, but I experienced my first ever miracle and first deliverances all in the same week of fasting. God was teaching me and encouraging me that when we die to self, we really come alive *in* Him and it is an amazing and fulfilling life!

Exercise be creative

The only way to set our mind on things of
God, is to talk to Him, read His word, listen
to Him, and obey. This is how we do
relationship with our Papa God and Jesus.

Please read Romans 8:5-17. What insights
did you find for yourself personally?

_____

_____

_____

_____

_____

_____

_____

_____

_____

_____

_____

_____

_____

_____

she will not be harmed because LOVE walks by her side

Isaiah 41:10

JM 19

So do not fear, for I am with you; do not be dismayed, for I am your God. I will strengthen you and help you; I will uphold you with my righteous right hand.

Isaiah 41:10

Dear Trusting One,

I have called you to be bold and courageous. You can do this because I am here with you and I will never leave you nor forsake you (Deuteronomy 31:8). You have nothing to fear because of who I AM in you.

Trust Me, the journey is hard but so rewarding. My purpose places a demand on you, but my burden is still lighter than walking this life alone; or worse, holding hands with the enemy.

My way is narrow but it is also higher and the view is spectacular from here. Stay close to Me and I will take you places you never thought were possible, because I love you.

Forever yours,

Jesus

Reflection & Response

Are you going through something life threatening? Maybe someone you know is?

Our faith can be rattled when it appears God is not answering our cries. We might pray for a certain outcome and it doesn't happen. In those times, I go to my default Scripture *Trust the Lord with all your heart and lean not on your own understanding but in all your ways acknowledge Him and He will make your paths straight.* Proverbs 3:5 Sometimes, however, that Scripture can feel futile.

But if I read Isaiah 41:10 and imagine that I am actually dying and about to come home, it takes on a whole different meaning. Death is not tragic if you know Jesus. Life is harder for those who are left behind. Jesus promised that in this world we will have trouble (John 16:33).

God is not a genie that gives us all the pleasures and comforts of life. Yes, He blesses us, but He also takes away (Job 1:21). It is wise to fear (revere) and obey Him (Proverbs 9:10) and we do this because we love Him; but remember, He loved us first (1 John 4:19). It's easy to question that love when He doesn't intervene in desperate situations. I don't know why He doesn't in those moments, but I do know that He asks us to partake in His suffering (1 Peter 4:13), to take up our cross and follow Him (Matthew 16:24-26). I also know that He has suffered tremendously for us and completely understands what we are going through and promises to never leave us.

If we are truly followers of Jesus, we will obey Him, and the assignment He has predestined for us to do (Jeremiah 29:11) - one that will give us a hope and a future, but we are not to fool ourselves and think that being a Christian is easy. The mere fact that we follow Jesus heightens the enemy's attack on us (1 Peter 5:8). However, we are never to lose heart. We have authority (Luke 10:19), and Jesus promises to be with us always (Isaiah 41:10).

Exercise be creative

2014 was a year of immense battles for me, but becoming an artist and painting for God was birthed and so much joy and blessings have come as a result.

What do you love to do?_____

_____

_____

Are you walking in the purpose God has for you? It's actually quite easy. Take what you are good at and love to do and use it to honor God. Give it back to Him.

Maybe you are still not sure? Spend some time with God this week and ask Him: "What do you want me to do?" Then obey.

Write down what He has been showing you this week. _____

_____

_____

_____

_____

_____

_____

she has
this hope
in
TRUTH
as an
anchor

Hebrews 6:19

We have this hope as an anchor for the soul, firm and secure. It enters the inner sanctuary behind the curtain, where our forerunner, Jesus, has entered on our behalf...

Hebrews 6:19-20

Dearest Bride,

I am your rock and salvation (Psalm 62:2); your ever present light in darkness. When you feel motion sickness from the storms, anchor your hope and trust in Me (Hebrews 6:19).

Follow Me to the inner sanctuary, the secret place where we can meet together face to face in intimacy. When you do this, you will feel grounded and secure. The longer you stay with Me the easier it is to face the storms of every day life.

In this life you will have trouble (John 16:33), but take heart, with Me you are an overcomer. Trust Me and you will know peace. I love you.

Forever yours,

Jesus

Reflection & Response

This is one of my favourite scriptures and I wear a necklace with an anchor on it to remind me that He anchors me when my circumstances become desperate. I also equate it with Jesus being like an anchor: solid, unchanging, and dependable. We can get out of the boat and not be shaken by the storms if we anchor ourselves in Christ and keep our gaze steady with His.

I personally know that if I spend time with Jesus, I receive revelation and guidance from Him that helps me through difficult and frightening situations. If I don't, however, I begin to panic and operate in the flesh losing hope and self control. I begin to make regretful choices or behave foolishly, ruminating on things I can't control.

Getting on my knees is the only way for me to rise above what looks like a hopeless situation. The more I hear what He has to say, the more I trust Him and let go. The more I let go, the more relaxed I become and allow Jesus to steer the ship.

Are you facing a difficult situation right now? What is it?_____

_____

_____

_____

_____

_____

Exercise be creative

Take time this week to ask God:

"Father, what do you think? Jesus, what do you love and Holy Spirit, what do you want to do?"

As you read Scripture and 3-4 devotionals each day, see if God is speaking to you in themes and write down what you think He might be saying pertaining to your situation. He loves to let us know, if we take the time to listen.

_____

_____

_____

_____

_____

_____

_____

_____

_____

_____

_____

she
lives in
joy &
peace,

creation
bursts
into
song
before
her

Isaiah 55:12

You will go out in joy and be led forth in peace, the mountains and hills will burst into song before you, and all the trees of the field will clap their hands.

Isaiah 55:12

Dear Adventurous One,

I want to take you on a journey beyond places you can see. This kind of passage requires that you trust Me fully, letting Me guide your every step. When you let go in this way, everything will fall into place and even nature around you will appear to be cheering you forward.

Don't be anxious about your finances, I will take care of you, even into old age (Matthew 6:25). Don't live to retire, live for Me, I won't let you down. This whole idea goes against your instinct for self-preservation, but I died to set you free from that oppressive thinking.

Live for Me and watch Me do it. I will never forsake you because I love you.

Forever yours,

Jesus

Reflection & Response

This Scripture is very dear to me. It was the one Papa God gave me, when I was seeking His heart about our plans to move to Edmonton and it popped up again when I questioned if we should be staying here after our 5 year plan was well and truly over. Initially, we thought we would be financially ahead by moving here, but in fact the opposite is true. Additionally, I yearn for the oceans in Australia and to bring my boys up with family; however Father God had other ideas. He brought us here to heal me and my marriage. I was an angry, bitter, and resentful woman. I spoke harshly and hastily and my husband said he found it hard to love me when I was so prickly all the time.

'Instead of the thorn bush, will be the evergreen pine tree.'

Originally, I equated this with Australia being like a thorn bush and Canada being the pine tree. However, after my fourth visit to 'Desert Streams,' a healing and deliverance ministry, I saw a picture that I hadn't noticed before on the way out. It was 'Spirit Island,' a famous island on Maligne Lake in Jasper, filled with pine trees. I distinctly heard God say to me: *Instead of being the thorn bush, you will be like the pine tree.* I welled up with tears as this was a desire of my heart.

Are you ready for Papa God to take you on a journey that may be completely different to what you expected? Are you ready to let go of working just to earn an income and begin living for the Lord? He can do immeasurably more than all you ask or imagine, if you let Him (Ephesians 3:20). _____

_____

Exercise be creative

God places the desires/will in you and works through you to act out those desires to fulfill His good purpose (Philippians 2:13).

If money was no object, what would you be doing? Don't be surprised if it is something creative. We are created in His image and He is the ultimate Creator.

_____

_____

_____

_____

Now take that idea, and how would you be doing it for God? _____

_____

_____

_____

_____

Ask God for His guidance, confirmation, and strength and be ready to bless Him with the gifts He has given you. Ask for wisdom, knowledge and understanding along the way.

love
delights
in her
and
she
is
transformed

Zeph 3:17

The Lord your God is with you, the Mighty Warrior who saves. He will take great delight in you; in His love He will no longer rebuke you, but will rejoice over you with singing.

Zephaniah 3:17

Dear Beautiful Child,

I am always with you and I will fight for you. I want you to rest in Me and trust Me. No temptation is too great for you (1 Corinthians 10:13), and no sin is too horrible for Me. I will forgive you always, if you ask Me to.

I am your Papa, your Daddy, and I delight in you. You are the apple of My eye (Deuteronomy 32:10). Let My love transform your heart and fill you up. I want to sing songs of love over you and hold you in My arms. Come to Me, experience Me, ask Me for what you need. I am always here waiting for you because I love you.

Forever yours,

Jesus

Reflection & Response

I know some people see God as an angry Father figure who wants to set up a bunch of rules and then punish us if we don't obey. This is far from who He is and Jesus came to demonstrate, by example, the character of His Father. He literally says, *'to know Me is to know My Father too. And from now on you will realise that you have seen Him and experienced Him.'* (John 14:6-7—TPT)

How do you perceive God?_____

_____

In Zephaniah 3:17, I actually see a very nurturing God who will fight to break down the walls we build just to get in and love us. He is our Mighty Warrior who wants to save us from self-destructive ways and sooth our soul with tender singing. He calls us to Himself; He pursues us, and is always waiting for us to come away with Him (Song of Songs 2:10).

When we choose to respond to His invitation, the ice around our heart begins to melt causing it to beat once again. To trust in love again, like we did when we were a small child. We need to turn to the right LOVE (God). The God who will never leave us or forsake us. The God who will always be there for us when we need Him, not the gods or idols that we set up, only to be disappointed. Only true LOVE will transform us.

Exercise be creative

Please download or go to YouTube and listen to 'Reckless Love' by Bethel Music & Stephany Gretzinger. Notice the words, *He chases me down, fights till I'm found, leaves the 99.* (Parable of the lost sheep—Matthew 18:12-14)

What other words have you discovered in this song that demonstrates the character and love of God for you? _____

_____

_____

_____

_____

_____

_____

_____

_____

_____

she

shines

like a

star

in the

night

Philippians 2:15

Do everything without grumbling or arguing, so that you may become blameless and pure, "children of God without fault in a warped and crooked generation." Then you will shine among them like stars in the sky as you hold firmly to the word of life...

Philippians 2:14-16

Dear Precious One,

I have set you apart for Me and I have work for you to do that will bring glory and honor to Me, and purpose and blessings for you (Ephesians 2:10). Do not get caught up in what the world values: money, title, and recognition; instead be transformed by Me and My thoughts about you (Romans 12:2). Hang on tightly to Me and you will begin to shine brightly in the lives of others and be a guiding light that bridges the gap between Me and them. All I need is your 'yes' and I will do the rest and you will see miracles unfold right before you.

I have called you to love and serve others without complaining. I know this is hard to do sometimes, so if you are annoyed by anyone or anything, bring your heart to Me and trust that I am working in and through all your situations (Romans 8:28). Do not worry, I love you.

Forever yours,

Jesus

Reflection & Response

Saying 'yes' to God is the most fulfilling life journey you will ever take. When we partner with God to do the work He has assigned specifically for us to do, we can't help but be blessed by success and purpose that not only transforms other people but our lives also.

Has there been a yearning in your heart to make a difference? What is it?_____

_____

In 2015, God was speaking to me a lot about fasting and the Holy Spirit highlighted the Scripture from Isaiah 58:6: *Is this not the kind of fasting I have chosen: to loose the chains of injustice and untie the cords of the yoke, to set the oppressed free and break every yoke?* As soon as I read it, I instantly knew that my heart was to see women set free: emotionally, physically, and spiritually. I didn't know what it looked like, but as Father God revealed my purpose to paint for Him, other opportunities began to unfold also.

It just takes asking God a simple question like: "What should I paint next God?" or "What can I do to help?" Along the way, it is important not to become sidetracked from your calling. You may feel like quitting because you are suddenly working with someone that you find difficult to be around. Or maybe you are becoming bored or tempted to take a path that will bring in more money. Keep your eyes on Jesus and if you are ever unsure whether you are doing His will, ask for confirmation.

Exercise be creative

My challenge to you this week is to take
what you love and ask God: "What do
you want me to do with this?" See where
He takes you and ask for confirmation
along the way.

Write your questions and His responses:

_____

_____

_____

_____

_____

_____

_____

_____

_____

_____

_____

_____

_____

_____

_____

_____

she

waits

in

hope

and

LOVE

hears

her

Micah 7:7

But as for me, I watch in hope for the Lord, I wait for God my Savior; my God will hear me.

Micah 7:7

Dear Lovely Daughter,

You can have full confidence that I am always here listening to everything you say, think, and feel.

I also see every situation you face, every difficulty you overcome, every tear you shed, and every frustration you endure.

Now I am waiting for you to come to Me with everything that is on your heart. You do not need to carry anything on your own. When you surrender and completely trust in Me, I will work all things out for your good (Romans 8:28), all you need to do is ask Me and then wait with hope.

I will not only transform your situation, but I will transform your life because I love you.

Forever yours,

Jesus

Reflection & Response

Throughout my walk with Jesus, there is one thing I am absolutely sure of: His timing, His ways, and His thoughts are very different from mine (Isaiah 55:8). That means, often I can not understand what He is doing and why He seems to take so long doing it.

I know the saying goes, a leopard can't change his spots, but the truth is, with God, all things are possible (Matthew 19:26), and maybe He is just working with tough, dried out, worn out, and uncooperative clay and it takes Him a little longer than we would like.

I think He must laugh at how impatient I am with His process, while He patiently works in my heart and situations, and that's only if I actually listen and obey.

When I do listen to Him, He begins to let me in on what He is doing little by little. This keeps me hanging onto hope as I wait for the transformation and changes to take place in my life and loved ones.

What changes would you like to see happen in your life?_____

_____

_____

_____

_____

Exercise be creative

This week, go to your Papa God and lay your heart out before Him and ask for what you are wanting. Do this every day and thank Him that He is already working in your life.

Ask Him also to show you what He is doing, so that you can keep holding onto hope that He is indeed listening to you.

Write down what He is showing you.

_____

_____

_____

_____

_____

_____

_____

_____

_____

_____

_____

_____

she can do anything because LOVE strengthens her

Philippians 4:13

I can do all things through Him who gives me strength.

Philippians 4:13

Dear Courageous One,

Because of who I AM, you have everything you need to overcome all obstacles in your way. Nothing is impossible for you because of My strength in you.

It is My joy to fulfill the desires of your heart (Psalm 37:4) when you ask Me. I also have wonderful plans for your life too. Sometimes your desires and My plans will line up and sometimes they won't, but when you ask for My direction and wait patiently for My answers, the plans I have will bring you hope and a wonderful future (Jeremiah 29:11).

My beautiful daughter, everything is going to be okay. Trust me, I want to do this *with* you because I love you.

Forever yours,

Jesus

Reflection & Response

I know stories of people who have overcome enormous difficulties and forged ahead being an inspiration for thousands. Liu Wei, a Chinese man who lost both arms after a childhood accident plays the piano beautifully with his feet. Walt Disney overcame poverty, Louis Zamperini overcame PTSD, Abraham Lincoln overcame chronic depression, Hellen Keller overcame loss of sight and hearing, and Oprah Winfrey overcame childhood abuse. These are just some famous people we know, but the list goes on and on in hidden and unknown people like you and me.

I struggled my whole life at school and failed almost every subject except for art. I had low self-esteem as a result. I never did pursue art because of fear and only in my late 40's I am finally pursuing art, a gift God has called me to. Had I chosen to walk closely with God from a young age, I might have pursued His calling a lot earlier, but He never wastes the road we have travelled. *Instead of your shame you will receive a double portion, and instead of disgrace you will rejoice in your inheritance. And so you will inherit a double portion in your land, and everlasting joy will be yours (Isaiah 61:7)*

I know God has the best plan for our life and He has already planted His gifts within us (Ephesians 2:10). It is our job to ask Him what He wants us to do.

How do we move forward from here in the plan and purpose God has for us?
We ask Him.

Exercise be creative

Write down the subject areas you loved at school the most, include any extra-curricular activities you were good at.

_____

_____

_____

Ask God to highlight which ones He wants to bring to your attention.

_____

_____

Ask Him to show you what He wants you to focus on as a job or career or perhaps what will bring Glory to Him.

Command every fear to go in the Name of Jesus that prevents you from moving forward in your true calling. Ask Him for the strength and courage you need to move forward. Let Him show you.

_____

_____

_____

_____

she hears, believes and miracles happen

Galatians 3:5

...does God give you His Spirit and work miracles among you by the works of the law, or by your believing what you heard? So, also Abraham "believed God, and it was credited to him as righteousness." Understand then, that those who have faith are children of Abraham.

Galatians 3:5-7

Dear Faithful One,

I not only came to give you eternal life but to give you the experience of the fullness of My Glory (Ephesians 3:19). My presence can take on so many forms and is only limited in your life by your thinking and beliefs.

Oh how I desire to unleash My goodness and power on you and equip you for every good work I have for you (Hebrews 13:21). You are not here to live for yourself, you are here to live for Me! And when you choose to do that and believe in Me, miracles will manifest in your life.

The choice is yours, either way, I love you.

Forever yours,

Jesus

Reflection & Response

In 2014, I began to feel a holy dissatisfaction. As I read the bible, I became more and more unsettled in my Spirit. If Jesus was real and everything He said is true, then shouldn't we be able to walk in miracles, signs, and wonders too? My conversion alone was an indication of the power of the Holy Spirit, so I wanted to go deeper. Then a friend, Kylie, introduced me to Heidi Baker's books and videos and I was undone by her testimonies. I spent that year getting up early and spending solid time with God and the doors began to open one after another. First He began dealing with my orphan spirit, then He began to teach me His ways.

It's been an incredible journey so far, but it does come with a cost. Being set apart for Him, can sometimes create distance with loved ones who don't agree or believe. That is really hard and the challenge is to continue to love them despite the differences and accept the journey *they* are on.

Have you ever experienced a miracle? _____

I used to do 'treasure hunts.' I would sit in the car before going to the grocery store and ask God who He wanted me to approach. I would ask what colour their clothes might be, the colour and length of their hair, and what age range I was looking for. I would ask for a name too. I would write down whatever came to my mind in faith. Once I met a lady who fit the description, even the name Harold was significant to her. As I was talking with her, I felt the Lord say her husband was unwell, and he was. He had just been released from the hospital. This woman started crying in disbelief at how intimately God knew her situation and I prayed with her.

Exercise be creative

The treasure hunt idea is pressing into the gift of words of knowledge and if you ever have time, look up Shawn Bolz who has this incredible gift with amazing stories.

Take a leap of faith and give listening to the voice of our Shepherd a chance. Ask God for the colour of her/his pants first and write down what comes to mind, then the colour of the top, the hair, and maybe an extra special feature, like a tattoo may come to mind or a certain necklace or glasses. Ask for a name too or something that only Jesus would know.

Take a leap, approach that person and just say, *"Hi, God highlighted you to me and I was wondering if the name (say name) means anything to you?"*

Now if it doesn't, that's okay, don't retreat in embarrassment, you are practicing and it takes time and practice to hear God's voice. Just say, *"That's okay, I just felt God wants to bless you because He wants you to know how much He loves you."*

You could also ask if they need prayer for anything. If this is too scary, you could try giving out a bible verse or give them my book as a way of blessing others. Watch some YouTube videos of Todd White. He's extremely bold and walks in miracles all the time.

she is still and LOVE fights for her

Exodus 14:14

The Lord will fight for you; you need only to be still.

Exodus 14:14

My Special Friend,

When you spend time with Me, you will often hear Me say: *'Peace...Trust Me.'* You will hear Me say this in the secret place of intimacy and connection. This is the place where you ask for what you need and as you face the world you will remain still and confident as you wait to see what I will do.

It is hard to trust someone you don't know, but if you seek to know Me as much as you are fully known by Me (1 Corinthians 8:3), you will be able to trust that I can do all things with you and for you. You will have a secure assurance that everything will be all right because I am fighting for you.

However, this kind of confidence and inner knowing comes with diligence. A daily walk with Me. When you get to know Me in this way, nothing will be able to shake you to the point of despair. You will remain on solid ground despite your circumstances.

Don't let your situations dictate your feelings, trust in Me. I love you.

Forever yours,

Jesus

Reflection & Response

Are you struggling with something that seems impossible for you to change right now?

Please explain.

_____

_____

_____

When we are faced with people we love who are lost or against us, or maybe a desperate situation that we can not change, life can feel impossible and hopeless. There is only one person who understands and promises never to leave us, Jesus. However, He promises us more than this, He says, *peace be still* to the storms of uncertainty and causes us to rise above our circumstances. He works a miracle in the atmospheric climate around us but also the struggles within us, if we trust and fix our eyes on Him (Matthew 14:22-33).

In these desperate situations, it is time to surrender and ask God to step in completely and trust Him with the process. More than anything, He wants to spend quality time with you; He wants you to get to know Him and how real He is.

If you are unsure that He is real, ask for something that would be meaningful to you. For example say, *"God if you are real, could you send a stranger to buy me a coffee tomorrow?"* We don't want to test our God (Matthew 4:7), but He does hear our heart.

Be specific. He longs to show you that He intimately knows and cares about you.

Exercise be creative

There are some struggles you have that you can not fix. Write them down on a piece of paper. Burn them up in the kitchen sink and say:

"Father God, I trust you with this situation completely. I let go and I am letting you fight for me on this one. Please give me the strength to go on without worrying about it any more. Help me with my unbelief when I feel oppressed by the anxiety of my situation. Thank you for taking care of it all."

Amen.

Write here any thoughts, feelings, or changes that might have happened for you this week.

_____

_____

_____

_____

_____

_____

_____

_____

she is
courageous
because
LOVE is
her
light,
salvation
and
stronghold

Psalm 27:1

The Lord is my light and salvation—whom shall I fear? The Lord is the stronghold of my life—of whom shall I be afraid?

Psalm 27:1

Dear Courageous One,

I have overcome Sin, Death, and Satan (1 Corinthians 15:56-57), therefore, nothing can harm you because I AM with you always. Keep your eyes steady on Me, I won't let you drown (Matthew 14:22-33). Trust Me, I can do what looks impossible for you. Rest in Me, I AM the peace you need in these times. Draw your strength from Me, I will give you the courage to face the world that looks uncertain.

The more time you spend with Me, the more you will hear My voice of reason in an unreasonable and unpredictable world. In this world you will have trouble, but be strong I have overcome everything (John 16:33) and I can do it for you, if you will let go and let Me.

Like the widow, don't stop asking Me to step in, your persistence will be rewarded (Luke 18:1-8). I love you.

Forever yours,

Jesus

Reflection & Response

What scares you the most in this life?_____

_____

_____

_____

This world we live in, is not our true home; we are aliens and strangers just passing through (Psalm 69:8, 1 Peter 2:11, 1 Chronicles 29:15). Jesus said, *My kingdom is not of this world... My kingdom is from another place* (John 18:36). When we have this perspective and we know Jesus has already overcome death, we have nothing to worry about. We will go home and be with Him one day and nothing and no one can take that away from us. So even if we die, we have that assurance. The rest is about listening to His voice, obeying it and trusting Him in this life.

Our purpose here is to stay connected to Jesus. It is a lifetime walk of listening, trusting and obeying Him. When we meet our Maker, our Husband (Isaiah 54:5), He will reward us and say, *Well done good and faithful wife* (Interpretation of Matthew 25:23).

What does: *God is my stronghold (Psalm 9:9-10),* mean? _____

_____

_____

_____

Exercise be creative

Blessed is the (woman) who remains steadfast under trial, for when (she) has stood the test (she) will receive the crown of life, which God has promised to those who love Him (James 1:12).

What trials is God asking you to remain steadfast in?_____

_____

_____

_____

_____

What do you think a crown of life means?

_____

_____

_____

_____

_____

Crown symbolises: power, legitimacy, victory, triumph, honor, glory, immortality , righteousness, and resurrection.

she
has
permission
to be messy
and LOVE
embraces
her
vulnerability

2 corintians 4:7

But we have this treasure in jars of clay to show that this all-surpassing power is from God and not from us.

2 Corinthians 4:7

Love of My Life,

I created you in My image; however, you are a small reflection of who I AM. I created you with limitations, vulnerabilities, and imperfections. I created you like this because I desire a deep connection with you, an intimate relationship. I want you to depend on Me. However, I know you would not if I created you to be all knowledgeable and powerful like Me.

Even now with all the limitations I have placed on people, they still choose to go their own way without Me. Except for you My beautiful one. You are reading this, because you seek Me. You seek to know what I think about you and what plans I have for you. So know this, I see your mess and your vulnerability and I love it, it keeps you humble and humility is one of My favourite traits.

Invite Me in, keep seeking My plans and My thoughts for you, and I will live in you and give you what you need in this life. I will fill the empty spaces in your heart, renew your strength (Isaiah 40:31), and love you in ways nobody else can.

Forever yours,

Jesus

Reflection & Response

No one is perfect; everyone falls short of the glory of God (Romans 3:23). In fact, if someone judges you, God is actually saying to them that their shortcomings are worse than yours (Matthew 7:3).

Are you happy with who you are?_____ Why or why not?_____

_____

_____

God created us messy, flawed, and imperfect for a reason. He wants us to rely on Him, to trust in Him and recognise that we need Him. Our flaws also keep us humble, but they are not meant to condemn us, put us to shame, or make us feel oppressed. He wants us to embrace ourselves, Him, and others. He wants us to love ourselves just as He does.

He wired each one of us uniquely and He sees how marvelous we are. He wants us to shout from the roof tops - *I praise you because I am fearfully and wonderfully made; your works are wonderful, I know that full well* (Psalm 139:14).

Despite our flaws, He actually looks into our eyes and says , *You are altogether beautiful, my darling; there is no flaw in you* (Song of Songs 4:7).

That might seem like a contradiction, but because of Jesus' atonement on the cross for our sins, God does not see our flaws anymore, even though they might still be there. And as we cleave to Him, we actually begin changing to become more like Him. This is a lifetime journey of growing from glory to glory (2 Corinthians 3:18).

Exercise be creative

Take some time this week and write out Psalm 139:14 and Song of Songs 4:7 on a sticky note and put it on your mirror in the bathroom and declare this every day:

I praise you God because I am fearfully and wonderfully made; your works are wonderful, I know that full well.

I am altogether beautiful, there is no flaw in me because of you Jesus.

After a week of doing this, write down how you feel or any changes you are experiencing within yourself as you declare these words over yourself.

_____

_____

_____

_____

Remember brainwashing happens over many years. It takes time to undo all the wrong perceptions you have about yourself, so be patient and keep going.

she has a
purpose
and delights
in LOVE
who
works
for her
good

Romans 8:28

And we know that in all things God works for the good of those who love Him, who have been called according to His purpose.

Romans 8:28

Dearest One,

I have amazing plans for you and a purpose that will bring fulfillment and joy to you and honor to Me (Jeremiah 29:11). Together, we can transform lives and be the love that so many are desperately seeking, but in all the wrong places. However, firstly, you need to know how much I **love** you. You need to believe *that* truth in the deep recesses of your soul. You also need to trust Me fully with everything: your relationships, your finances and your health.

Understand this fundamental truth. I am **always** working for your good.

Even when darkness envelops you, I am working for your good, even if it doesn't feel like I am... I am. I AM GOOD and I'm working it out for you, if you let Me. I am asking that you surrender it ALL in order for Me to do this properly.

Sometimes you will think I am bringing you harm when it is the enemy. The enemy comes to steal, kill, and destroy (John 10:10), so if that is happening in your life, that is not Me. But if you are experiencing inconvenience, that *could* be Me working for your good. Only walking closely with Me will help you discern the difference.

As confusing as it all may seem, know this: I love you.

Forever yours,

Jesus

Reflection & Response

Are you asking God to work out everything for you? It's only in the asking do we then receive (Matthew 7:7). God wants to do a good thing in you, for you, and through you.

What good work would you like Papa God to do *in* you? _____

_____

For me, I wanted God to change my heart and I would always pray: *God create in me a clean heart and renew a right spirit in me (*Psalm 51:10).

What good work do you want God to do *for* you? _____

_____

_____

I want God to work in the hearts and minds of my loved ones and restore broken relationships. I also want the art I produce to sell well and I would also like to be debt free.

What good work do you want God to do *through* you?_____

_____

_____

I want God to work through me to touch people's lives in significant and healing ways. I want to see people restored in their identity with Him, like He has been restoring me.

The work *in* you is the most important one because without a healthy self-love, we can't possibly love God and others.

Exercise be creative

On a sticky note write Psalm 51:10. Add it to the other sticky notes around your mirror to remind yourself morning and night to ask God to continue transforming you and filling you up with His love.

Remember that it can take years to know and believe how valuable, worthy, and loved you are. There is no rush, take your time in this season of self love. Also know that this can be a lifetime progression as well, but there will come a moment when it will start to click and you will be ready to love on others.

If you are already in that process of loving, accepting, and approving of yourself, then it is time to ask God to move through you with a purpose He has for you.

What season are you in? Write down any insights you might have.

_____

_____

_____

_____

_____

she is a princess in the kingdom of light

Colossians 1:12

...and giving joyful thanks to the Father, who has qualified you to share in the inheritance of His holy people in the Kingdom of light.

Colossians 1:12

My Sweet Princess,

You are a child of Papa God (1 John 3:1), a child of the King of Kings - that makes you His princess in His Kingdom. You are qualified to be with Him because *We* paid the price and adopted you. If you ever feel that you are not good enough to be with Him or to represent Him in this life, let Me tell you, you are. You are qualified, not because of anything you have done, but because of what *We* have done *for* you.

Nobody is better, more worthy, or more qualified than you in My Kingdom. I am not calling you to perform and be perfect; I am calling you into an intimate relationship with Me, to be united with Me, to walk and talk with Me, and to live *for* Me and not yourself (2 Timothy 1:9).

When you do life with Me in this way, transformation will happen within you. I am not asking you to change you, I am asking you to rest in Me, lay your burdens down and ask for My help. Allow Me to do all the heavy lifting. You just rest in the knowledge that I love you.

Forever yours,

Jesus

Reflection & Response

Are you able to accept that you are Papa God's princess, that you are royalty in His Kingdom and qualified to walk with Him in this life?_____

_____

It may appear like a fantasy, but the bible is a living, breathing spiritual book (2 Timothy 3:16-17) and not just a factual account of what happened over 2,000 years ago. Jesus spoke in parables all the time to illustrate a point but over the centuries we have lost the ability to seek deeper truths through the poetic art of storytelling. God created us to be a spirit and our bodies were made to carry it (1 Corinthians 6:19). Our body is just dust without His spiritual breath within us, (Genesis 2:7) He knew us before we were even born (Jeremiah 1:5).

We are only here for a short time and then we will go to be with the King of kings and Lord of lords in His Kingdom and we will stand before His throne and give an account of everything we have said and done on this earth (2 Corinthians 5:10, Matthew 12:36).

This is not designed to frighten us, because God is LOVE (1 John 4:7-8), but it does remind us that we need to be held accountable to Him and revere Him, listen to Him and obey. It's okay if we stumble and fall, we just ask for forgiveness and He forgives us. He then picks us up, dusts us off and says *"you are doing great, don't give up, keep going."* He's not asking you to be His Court Jester, He's asking you to be His Daughter and just wants a relationship with you.

Exercise be creative

Write down the ingredients needed to have a good relationship with someone.

_____

_____

_____

_____

_____

Has people in your life let you down? Write down how they have contaminated your hope in a good relationship.

_____

_____

_____

_____

_____

Jesus loved people but He didn't entrust himself to them, for He knew them (John 2:24). He often walked away to spend time with His Father (Luke 5:16). He is our example of what we need to do also. Love God first, spend loads of time with Him and then go and love others. Spending time with God is more important than spending time with anyone else, even at church.

she
kept on
knocking
and the
door
opened

matthew 7:7

Ask and it will be given to you; seek and you will find; knock and the door will be opened to you.

Matthew 7:7

Highly Favoured One,

I am always here waiting for you to talk to Me and ask Me for My help. I can help in ways you never dreamed was possible (Ephesians 3:20). You limit Me in your life because you do not ask or you ask with wrong motives (James 4:3), but I am faithful to those who persevere (Luke 18:1-8) and believe (Mark 9:23-25).

Pursue Me with your heart and watch how I respond. I long to give you good gifts (Matthew 7:11) and reveal Myself to you in unique and intimate ways.

Come to Me and let Me show you and tell you marvelous secrets you do not know (Jeremiah 33:3). I am longing to take you on an even deeper journey because I love you.

Forever yours,

Jesus

Reflection & Response

Do you find it hard to ask for help? Maybe you are worried people will say no or you have experienced too much rejection to ask any more? Write down your thoughts.

_____

_____

_____

There is plenty of Scripture that demonstrates that God wants us to ask Him for His help and for good things. However, sometimes I feel like He is never going to give me the desires of my heart because I have been waiting for so many years. Then I am reminded of other characters in the bible who waited 25 years or longer and I am reassured that God is faithful and just maybe the good work He is doing in me, needs to be completed first. That definitely could take some time.

There are other times when He answered a prayer by the next day because I asked Him to. Like the bangle He gave me to encourage me that I was indeed a good mom (story found on page 45). God is mysterious; however, we can't always fully understand how or why He works in the way He does. One thing is for sure, He loves us, He will never leave us, and He desires a relationship with us.

What do you think?_____

_____

_____

_____

Exercise be creative

Write down all the things you would like Papa God to do for you. Be specific. Some might be answered within the week and some might take years. Tick off the ones He answers within the week and be encouraged.

_____

_____

_____

_____

_____

_____

_____

_____

_____

_____

_____

_____

_____

_____

_____

LOVE

delights

in her

and

calms

all

her

fears

Zeph 3:17

The Lord your God is with you, the Mighty Warrior who saves. He will take great delight in you; in His love He will no longer rebuke you, but will rejoice over you with singing.

Zephaniah 3:17

My Beautiful Princess,

I am here for you always. I take pleasure in who you are because I created you exactly as you are. You are so unique and special and I adore you. I want you to come higher and see yourself as I do, delightful and perfect in your imperfection.

Do not be afraid of how others may see you. Do not entertain any other thoughts about you, accept Mine. Stay with Me, learn from Me, believe Me when I say you are wonderful (Psalm 139:14), learn to love you as I do. Only then, will you be able to love others and see *them* as I do.

Broken people hurt others. You live in a broken world and it can be a scary place. Draw your strength and courage from Me. Soak yourself in My thoughts and words and then you will be able to love others in their brokenness rather than be offended by them.

Remember, I am especially fond of you and I love you.

Forever yours,

Jesus

Reflection & Response

Who do you think you are? Ever heard someone say that to you in anger? My reply is always, *"I'm a child of God."*

Write down who you think you are. _____

_____

Sometimes my youngest boy displays all kinds of anger at home and at school. A lot of hostility rises up as he fights for his place in the family with two older brothers. I sometimes get frustrated with his behaviour and I need to keep remembering what he was like as a little child, he was filled with so much joy. Then I would speak life over him by saying, *"you are not an angry boy, you are filled with joy."* I would then go into great detail about what he was like when he was little. I would remind him that, that is who he really is.

You are created unique and special and when the layers of hurt, rejection, shame, disappointment, and hostility are removed, you are left with who God created you to be. His joyful, curious, accepting, trusting, non-judging child.

This is the person He wants you to rediscover again. However, it can only be done over time and in deep connection with Him. Few people travel this narrow road with Jesus and as a result the world remains a broken and hostile place. Our place of rest and peace is within His arms and we have to fight the distractions and temptations around us, to get to the secret place with Him.

Exercise be creative

Write down all the good things about your
personality that make you unique and
special.

_____

_____

_____

_____

_____

This is God's signature stamp on you. He
fused you together to be like this.

Write all the things you love to do.
Don't think about whether you are good at
them or not, that is irrelevant.

_____

_____

_____

_____

_____

These are the gifts God has placed within
you. He loves watching you play with
them,. Continue to do so irrespective of
what you think others may think. The
more you enjoy His gifts, the better you
will get.

she can fly because she is recklessly and unconditionally LOVED

(Galatians 2:20)

I have been crucified with Christ and I no longer live, but Christ lives in me. The life I now live in the body, I live by faith in the Son of God, who loved me and gave Himself for me.

Galatians 2:20

My Precious Bride,

I am asking you to no longer identify with yourself and what *you* want but to identify with *Me* and what *I* think and feel about you and your life. I love you so much that I died to take away your shame, your sicknesses, and your hurts. I died so that you could come to My Father without blemish or blame (2 Corinthians 5:21).

You are not perfect but you are perfectly loved just the way you are and We don't see your sin, We only see *you* and We want an intimate relationship with you.

Come fly away with Me, you are free to be completely yourself. Just. As. You. Are. There is no condemnation or judgment (Romans 8:1) because I love you.

Forever yours,

Jesus

Reflection & Response

What do you think it means to be unconditionally loved?_____

_____

What was your upbringing like? Did you feel unconditionally loved by your parents?

_____

_____

What things do you think you need to do to feel accepted by others?_____

_____

_____

My experiences growing up were not based on unconditional love. I didn't measure up to my mother's ideal and I didn't feel any emotional or physical intimacy from my dad. I easily took these feelings of rejection and low self-worth into my relationships and hoped that they could fill the empty spaces in my heart, but they couldn't. Often I became hostile, hoping to manipulate others into giving me what I wanted. I didn't have the emotional maturity to understand that no one was responsible for making me feel good. All I knew was that I was not enough and my partner was not enough either. In fact, it wasn't until I went to Jesus in a deeper way, did I begin to realise my self-worth and how utterly loved, accepted, and valued I am.

It's been a five year journey and I know I still have a long way to go, but I have come a long way knowing that my Papa God created me unique, loves me unconditionally and accepts me exactly as I am. I now understand that my purpose is to love others and not try to get it from them. God is the source of love and I now go to Him for it.

Exercise be creative

You will need:

Red paper, scissors, and a pen.

Take the red paper and cut out ten small love hearts. Write a special love note from Jesus on each of the love hearts.

Some ideas:

You are utterly loved, I embrace who you are, you are special and unique, I want to hold you tightly, let me kiss your pain away, tell me everything—I'm here for you.

Write some of your own ideas:

_____

_____

_____

_____

_____

_____

_____

Hide these love notes around your personal belongings, so that you will come across them during the week.

she
will
not
be
shaken
unfailing
LOVE
promises
her
peace
and
compassion

(Isaiah 54:10)

Though the mountains be shaken and the hills be removed, yet My unfailing love for you will not be shaken nor my covenant of peace be removed, says the Lord, who has compassion on you.

Isaiah 54:10

My Special Daughter,

I long to give you the unshakable peace you desire and need in this world. Spend time with Me and give Me all your burdens. Rest in Me and learn from Me, I will exchange your troubles for my easy yoke of friendship (Matthew 11:28).

Surrender it all! All your anxieties, all your fears, all your hurts, and all your concerns. If you let go, then I can move in and do something wonderful in your life.

Trust Me, I really do care about you (1 Peter 5:7). Come and sit with Me just for a while and share what's on your heart and what you need. I will never step in and just assume. Like the blind man who came to Me, I still asked, "what do you want Me to do for you?" (Mark 10:51) I say this, because I always have and always will desire a relationship with you, because I love you.

Forever yours,

Jesus

Reflection & Response

It stands to reason that if we can not be shaken or get anxious in our circumstances, then peace will be ours.

How do you behave when you are feeling anxious or triggered?_____

_____

_____

I can often ruminate about an issue. I just won't stop thinking about it. I will try to come up with solutions in my head even though I know I can't change people or my situation. When my buttons are pushed, I might get really angry, my heart will be beating fast, and I either want to fight or run away. I might contact a friend or see a counsellor and this can help give me perspective, but it still might not change anything. Additionally, I don't want to burden my friends, and a counsellor can be expensive and unhelpful in a spontaneous and desperate moment.

Sometimes, I shut out my problems by watching a movie or eating chocolate. Some people might use substances to escape their pain or situation, or run to the next exciting thing, or keep themselves extremely busy. However, running away from our hurts or ourselves doesn't actually work or fix anything, but running to Jesus does.

Relationships are very important to me, so knowing that Jesus is a person who is actually there for me ALL the time, gives me the hope and strength I need to carry on. When He encourages me, I know all things are possible, and that gives me peace.

Exercise be creative

This week, if you come across a stressful situation and you feel yourself getting angry, I want you to observe what your body is doing. Usually your heart will start beating faster.

All emotions are temporary and they do move on. So try objectively talking to yourself about what your body is doing.

Write down your symptoms when you are feeling anxious, overwhelmed, or angry.

_____

_____

_____

_____

_____

Ask Jesus to step in and calm your heart and your mind. Sometimes I need to walk away and find a quiet place and talk to Jesus about what is on my heart. Then I imagine laying it all at His feet and saying, *"I trust you with this Jesus."*

If you are feeling anxious this week, no matter where you are, even if you have to go to the washroom, go and calm your body, take deep breaths, and talk to Jesus.

she has
life and
peace
because
she sets
her
mind
on
wings
of
LOVE

(Romans 8:6)

The mind governed by the flesh is death, but the mind governed by the Spirit is life and peace.

Romans 8:6

My Child,

In this world, there is so much vying for your attention: money, sex, and all kinds of pleasurable distractions. The flesh craves to be satisfied by what the world offers, but the Spirit in you wants to rise above these empty promises.

When you set your mind on My words, your spirit begins to hunger for more of what I have for you. I offer what the world can not (John 14:27), things that your soul and spirit really crave: love, joy, peace, kindness, gentleness, and tenderness (Galatians 5:22). I offer you an abundant life (John 10:10).

Come to Me, spend time with Me and experience exactly how full and rich your life can become. I love you.

Forever yours,

Jesus

Reflection & Response

What pleasures do you seek in this life? _____

_____

_____

_____

Does pursuing them make you feel at peace? _____

_____

I used to be a serial dater. I went from one boyfriend to the next trying to get the love and attention I thought I needed to feel full. All it did though, was bring temporary relief and long term frustration, anxiety and disappointments. I was deeply troubled but I didn't know how to heal. I thought it was because I hadn't found the right person yet. I blamed my unhappiness on external factors rather than looking at the roots of my pain. The abundant life Jesus has for us can not be found in the pleasures the world offers or in a specific person. The peace and contentment we really crave only comes when we really accept and love ourselves exactly as we are. Feeling absolutely comfortable in our own skin is not easy but can happen when we set our mind on Papa God and what He thinks about us.

I now know how much He loves me and created me wonderful and unique and when I pursue Him through prayer, scriptures, and devotionals, He begins to unfold His love and purpose for me. The more time I give to Him, the more I receive on so many levels (Luke 6:38).

Exercise be creative

This week I challenge you to not reach for the thing you usually reach for to make you feel good.

Instead, try listening to some worship music and ask God to take the temptation you are feeling away. Then ask God to speak to you and randomly open your bible and see what He has to say. Now, open a devotional book and read what it says. Write down what you think God is trying to say to you.

_____

_____

_____

_____

_____

_____

_____

_____

Do this every day if you can. Keep a journal and record what God might be saying to you. Notice any themes He might be revealing to you.

she

loves

without

expectation

luke 6:35

But love your enemies, do good to them, and lend to them without expecting anything back. Then your reward will be great, and you will be children of the Most High...

Luke 6:35

My Darling,

I am calling you higher to the kind of love that does not operate in this world (John 15:19), a love that goes against every logic you were brought up with and surrounded by. This kind of love is a dying to self and becoming alive in Me (Galatians 2:20). You can only achieve this kind of love by spending much time with Me and learning about how much *you* are utterly and unconditionally loved.

This is the highest calling of all and it is extremely hard, but the rewards are beyond anything you could possibly understand. Come to Me daily for the strength, wisdom and heart you will need to love others without expecting anything in return.

Ask for My help every day, and remember, no matter how many times you may fail at this, I love you.

Forever yours,

Jesus

Reflection & Response

Think of a family member that triggers you and that seems to push all your buttons, or that hurts you. Do you think it is possible to love them without expecting anything back from them?_____

What could you do to show that person love? _____
_____
_____

What about someone outside the family? Maybe you work with them. How could you show love to them even though they are not kind back?_____
_____

Being asked to love someone who can't reciprocate that love, or who is unkind, is the highest calling God could ask of someone and it's hard, sometimes impossible. First, He needs to deal with our own wounded heart and show us how much He loves and adores us, then he needs to teach us to focus on Him rather than ourselves; then He will ask us to love someone close to us even though it may not be reciprocated. Sometimes letting go of all expectations from our spouse, parents, or siblings can be the only thing left to do, and sticking around and staying kind could be enough demonstration of our love for them without doing much else.

Loving someone without expectation of it returned is almost impossible and I constantly need to go to my Papa God and ask Him to remove my hurts and create in me a clean heart so that I can keep going without bitterness and resentment. I have to lay my heart open before my Daddy God and weep, then forgive, release, and bless that person. Then I get up and try again.

Exercise be creative

1. This week, ask God to bring the right person to your mind that you have a hard time showing love and kindness to.

2. Spend time before Jesus and lay down all the hurts that person has caused you and how each one made you feel.

3. Forgive each hurt they caused you. Say to Papa God *"I forgive (person's name), I release them and I bless them."*

4. Ask God how He wants you to show love to that person. Act upon the thought that He gives you.

5. Be obedient.

Write down who He asked you to love and what He asked you to do. Also write down if anything good came from being obedient. Remember, don't expect anything in return, your obedience to God is good enough to receive your reward in this life or the next.

_____

_____

_____

_____

she can fly because LOVE strengthens her

(Isaiah 40:31)

But those who hope in the Lord will renew their strength like the eagles, they will run and not grow weary, they will walk and not grow faint.

Isaiah 40:31

Dearest Love,

Come to Me if you are burdened and I will give you rest (Matthew 11:28). This is My promise to you and My word does not return to Me empty (Isaiah 55:11). I can do more than just give you rest, I can breathe My life into you that will give you the strength to soar above the confusion and fears of this world.

Trust in Me and have hope, I can do the impossible in your life (Luke 1:37). Don't be anxious about anything, leave everything that is worrying you at My feet. I can take care of it all, if you will let Me, (Philippians 4:6) because I care deeply about you and every detail of your life (1 Peter 5:7).

When you walk through life without a care or a worry because of your trust in Me, not only will you be able to run, but it will feel like you can fly. Let go, I've got this because I love you.

Forever yours,

Jesus

Reflection & Response

Imagine you are carrying a super big and heavy television up a very steep flight of stairs. It is awkward and you are anxious and scared because if you drop it, you would damage it and the money and time you invested in getting it would be wasted. Now, imagine someone you know and trust comes along and takes the television from you and carries it for you. How would this make you feel? _____

_____

_____

Imagine that television is your finances, your relationships, your health, or some other enormously difficult situation. Imagine Jesus is standing right in front of you asking you to pass that enormous issue over to Him to carry because He is more than capable and is trustworthy with your important but difficult situation.

Sometimes my circumstances are too big to handle and all I can do is ask Jesus to take care of them. That doesn't mean He fixes everything right away; in fact sometimes the process unfolds slowly because He is showing me something I need to learn. Like going to University, it takes years of learning before we are qualified in that area.

Have you every watched a removalist carry something big and heavy that is precious to you and you stand there watching in agony, just wanting to somehow take over? Often, I grab that big television back again because I can't seem to let go and trust that it is safe in Jesus' capable hands. Letting go and trusting, can be the hardest thing; but the more I do it, in the quiet place with Him, the easier it becomes.

Exercise be creative

1. This week, find a backpack and fill it up with five cans of baked beans. Label the cans with burdens you feel. If you don't have any cans, just find some heavy things to carry around.

2. Try to carry the backpack around for an hour, maybe while cooking the dinner or cleaning the house.

3. After 20 minutes take out a can and imagine laying it at the feet of Jesus.

4. Do this every 20 minutes until the backpack is empty.

Write down how you felt in your body and emotionally during this exercise.

_____

_____

_____

_____

_____

_____

_____

_____

_____

she hears LOVE whisper in her heart

1 Kings 19:12

After the earthquake came the fire, but the Lord was not in the fire. And after the fire came a gentle whisper.

1 Kings 19:12

Dear Desirable One,

I am not in the obvious places, I am in your heart. I do not force and I am not loud. I gently nudge and invite you into My space within you. It takes a lot of practice in the secret place to learn the sound of My gentle whispers (John 10:27). I speak in an accent few understand because they do not spend enough time with Me. Close friends understand what I am saying but even they will only know in part (1 Corinthians 13:9).

There are three voices competing for you attention: the enemy's, Mine, and yours. To be sure, they all sound like you, but the enemy's voice wants to tempt, accuse, and confuse you and he will always appeal to your flesh. You have authority to command it to leave in My name. By contrast, My voice will always line up with the Word and bring you peace, when you are unsure if I am speaking, ask for confirmation; I love communicating with you. Your voice is your soul (will and flesh) or it's your spirit which is aligned with Mine (Hebrews 4:12). Who you listen to the most becomes your voice also, so choose your input wisely (1 Corinthians 15:33, Proverbs 13:20).

The more time you spend with Me and My words and obey, the more you will operate in the spirit and not the flesh, then you will begin to hear My voice more clearly. I know it can be difficult, but remember this, I love you always.

Forever yours,

Jesus

Reflection & Response

We are all influenced by the voices of our past and in our life today. They may be parents, teachers, friends, books, media, and television. What voices are you influenced by the most today? _____

_____

The only voice I want to be influenced by is God's. Admittedly, I don't read a lot of secular books, nor do I follow the news, or watch much television. I am also careful with what company I keep because I know how easily influenced I can be. Some would say that this is not balanced, but I live for Jesus and He's the only one who can balance me in an unstable world.

Learning to hear God's voice clearly has been one of my hearts desires for years. I marvel at the way Shawn Boltz can hear God's voice so clearly, many people are won over to Jesus because this gift touches them in a personal way. It demonstrates how real Jesus is and people feel fully known and loved by God.

There are many examples where Jesus had knowledge about people that transformed them. Jesus knew Nathanael and what he was doing (John 1:47) and He knew about the life of the Samaritan woman at the well (John:1:4-26). This gift Jesus walked in had a huge impact on people's lives. Having the gift of hearing God's voice connects us to His heart for us and others; however, it takes discipline, courage, and obedience to fine tune it.

I used to practice by doing treasure hunts with Pastor Gary. Now I am part of 'Warrior Women—fighting for families' on Facebook and usually once a month we have a 'Soaking Saturday,' whereby we pray over individuals and practice hearing God's voice for them.

Exercise be creative

Receiving words of knowledge about another person, often just feels like an idea, thought, or picture you see in your head. It's information about them. It let's them know that God sees them. I am never sure if it is me or God placing it there and the only way to find out, is to approach that person with what I saw or felt. Prophecy is slightly different, it is more an encouraging word for a person or seeing something for their future. One must be careful with the latter and ask God for confirmation before releasing words about people's future.

Read — Colossians 2:3 on words of knowledge.

1 Corinthians 14:3 on prophecy.

Write down your understanding of both and how they are different.

_____

_____

_____

Think of someone you know and ask God for a scripture for that person, see if one pops in your mind, or randomly look in your bible. If it seems appropriate, write it out and give it to them in faith. At the very least, it will be encouraging.

she
is
strong
and
powerful
she
endures
and is
patient

Colossians 1:11

...being strengthened with all power according to His glorious might so that you may have great endurance and patience...

Colossians 1:11

Dear Valuable Child,

Come to Me and I will give you the wisdom and understanding you need for your life. Get to know who I have called you to be, who you actually are in Me. Good, pure, and delightful (1 Peter 2:9).

In this world, you will have trouble (John 16:33). People will hurt and disappoint you; I knew this and never entrusted Myself to them (John 2:24). That's why I say guard your hearts (Proverbs 4:23) and be as shrewd as snakes but as innocent as doves (Matthew 10:16).

Instead, come to Me for the answers; I will tell you what's up ahead and what to hope for. I will pour into you the love you need to keep going and I will give you the patience you need to wait for the promises I have made.

Don't give up in doing well, you are surrounded by saints and angels and We are all watching and cheering you on in this life (Hebrews 12:1). The journey may seem long to you, but it is a nano second in the company of eternal life. Keep your eyes fixed on Me and do not lose heart (Hebrews 12:1-3). I love you.

Forever yours,

Jesus

Reflection & Response

Have you been terribly hurt by others? Are you afraid to connect with people or let your guard down? Explain how you protect yourself from hurts and disappointments.

_____

_____

_____

If I ever felt hurt or rejected by my husband, I would become verbally hostile. I realise now, I was trying to hurt back. Discovering my self-worth through the unconditional love of Jesus significantly refined me and over the years, He has taught me many lessons. The words I speak have been my steepest learning curve. He taught me how to temper my tongue and go to Him and be sad instead of mad with my husband. God walked me through the theme of offense; He kept providing offensive situations for me to learn from until I was no longer offended. I have always wanted to be a better wife, mother, friend, and person, so I keep asking God to teach me. If I stay in Him, I will learn how to endure and be patient in difficult times and I will learn to live by the Spirit and not the flesh. My flesh wants to run away and self indulge in pleasures that make me feel momentarily good but ultimately send me down a destructive path.

In Him I have wisdom that helps me make the right choices despite my feelings. Don't get me wrong, this is a life long journey of struggle and growth.

It's okay to be guarded, people can be hurtful, but we are to respond in kindness even when people are thoughtless (Proverbs 15:1). The only way we can do this is to spend lots of time with Jesus. Having a relationship with Him can make crooked paths straight within us (Isaiah 45:2). He can smooth out our prickles and teach us to love the unlovely.

Exercise be creative

Sometimes we are struggling through something that has been going on for many years. It can become very discouraging and we can lose hope if we do not go back to Papa God and ask for encouragement.

Write down the things that you have been struggling with for a very long time.

_____
_____
_____
_____

Write down what you want God to do, be specific. _____

_____
_____

This week ask God for some encouragement. Write down how He encouraged you.

_____
_____
_____
_____

her
words
are
sweet
like
honey

proverbs 16:24

Gracious words are honeycomb, sweet to the soul and healing to the bones.

Proverbs 16:24

Dear Sweet Child,

Your tongue has the power to give life or destroy others, including yourself (Proverbs 18:21). How healthy your heart is will determine what words you say (Matthew 12:34). If you have been hurt, rejected, or bitterly disappointed over the years then bitterness and discontent will be the platform from which you speak. The only way to turn your words around, is to turn your heart to Me.

Firstly, you need to deeply forgive each person that has hurt you, including yourself. Picture each person and talk to them as if they are really there. Tell them what they did and how it made you feel. Label any shame they caused you and forgive each grievance on the list they did against you. In addition, ask Me for forgiveness for each hurtful thing you have said or done to yourself and others.

Secondly, acknowledge the shame you have been carrying all these years. This shame produces anger, fear, and rage. It is not yours. I took your shame when I died for your sins (Hebrews 12:2). Lay it all at my feet.

Thirdly, come to Me. Drink in the words I speak over you. Get to know my heart for you. It will heal you and in time, your mouth will be a wellspring of living waters for others (John 7:38). Most importantly, never forget that I love you deeply.

Forever yours,

Jesus

Reflection & Response

Is it easy or difficult for you to return a kind word when people are mean? _____
_____

Unfortunately, it is the people we are the closest to that we hurt the most. Words can cut deep and over time we can really wound the ones we love. God wants us to use our words to build others up, not tear them down. Even more so, He wants us to soak in His words because they are alive and active, sharper than a double edge sword; they truly test our hearts, and minds and help us to grow up in Him (Hebrews 4:12).

When it comes to words, what was your upbringing like?

_____
_____
_____

Hurts from our parents and bad role modeling can really damage us and cause us to walk in brokenness too. Generational sins are real and everything gets passed along - the good, the bad, and the ugly. We can break habitual cycles though if we really want to. A lot of work, support, and time in Scripture and with Jesus has helped me enormously over the years. Forgiving our parents and anyone else who has hurt us while growing up is step number one and mandatory to healing.

Who do you need to forgive?_____
_____

Often we need to do this more than once because experiencing deliverance through forgiveness can be a process.

Exercise be creative

This week find three small containers.

Have some white buttons in one, and black buttons in the other, and the middle one stays empty.

I went to 'Michaels,' a craft store and found little glass containers and white and black glass buttons. You can use anything you like though.

For every kind or encouraging word you say, you put a white button in the middle container. For every harsh thing you say, put a black button in the centre.

The aim is to have more white buttons than black. The people you are living with can help you do this. Keep it light and fun and be patient with yourself. If you keep trying and don't give up, you will get there... eventually.

Write down your experiences.

_____

_____

_____

_____

she

is

wise

and

carries

kindness

(Proverbs 31:26)

She speaks with wisdom and faithful instruction is on her tongue.

Proverbs 31:26

Dearest Love,

To fear God is to be wise and to know Him is to have understanding (Proverbs 9:10). I am not talking about being scared of My Father, I am talking about the awe and greatness of God who passionately wants to give you good things (Matthew 7:11). However, receiving good things can only come from a place of obedience, and obedience happens more easily when you have the gift of the fear of the Lord (Isaiah 11:2-3).

If a child steals candy from a store, does any good come of that, apart from his flesh being immediately gratified? But, when a child obeys and makes good choices, he will find favour in his parents eyes and he will know peace and joy.

Come walk with Me and learn from Me. Ask Me for the gifts of the Spirit (Romans 12:6-8, 1 Corinthians 12:8-10). I have so much to tell you (Jeremiah 33:3). The closer you walk with Me each day, the more pure your heart will become (Psalm 51:10); the more pure your heart the more you will walk and talk in wisdom and impact the world around you for good.

I know this seems like a lot, so keep it simple for now and just know that I love you.

Forever yours,

Jesus

Reflection & Response

Two days ago a word came to my mind, '*Sofia.*' I even said it out loud a couple of times. I knew it was a woman's name but for some reason I also knew it meant something else, but I let it go and thought nothing of it.

Last night, I couldn't sleep well as I was struggling with thoughts of my marriage. In the morning, I was feeling incredibly tempted to throw the towel in and do something foolish. I said to God, "I really need lots of encouragement today." As soon as I got up I checked my phone and a pastor's wife in Uganda was checking in with me on Facebook. We spent a long time texting each other, she was very encouraging.

After walking the children to school, I started writing this book. I was reflecting on hearing God's voice (1 Kings 19:12) and writing about Shawn Bolz. I accidently came across one of his course websites and there was the word *SOFIA*, which is the Greek word for *WISDOM*. Wisdom is one of the gifts of the Holy Spirit (1 Corinthians 12:8) and it has served me well at significant cross roads in my life. Shawn describes SOFIA as having the knowledge to regulate one's relationship with God and SOFIA is a wisdom that is related to goodness. Goodness is also a fruit of the Spirit (Galatians 5:22). Needless to say, I was very encouraged by God to walk in His wisdom that day.

God delights in blessing us with His special gifts, but it doesn't come suddenly. These gifts come over a long period of time, through much practice. Walking with Jesus is definitely a journey not a destination, and testimony comes as a result of the transition, the waiting and the trials.

If you want the gifts and the fruit, eagerly desire them and persist in asking for them (1 Corinthians 14:1).

Exercise be creative

Read: Romans 12:6-8 and 1 Corinthians 12:8-10.

Write down the gifts of the Spirit:

_____

_____

_____

_____

Read: Galatians 5:22.

Write down the fruit of the Spirit.

_____

_____

_____

_____

What is the difference between the gifts and the fruit? _____

_____

_____

_____

_____

she
has
hope
and
waits
for
LOVE

psalm 130:5

I wait for the Lord, my whole being waits, and in His word I put my hope.
Psalm 130:5

My Dear One,

Sometimes I ask my children to persevere in prayer and wait.

Abraham waited 25 years before Our promises were fulfilled in his life. Moses spent 40 years in the desert before he stepped into Our calling. Joseph knew his calling through a dream We gave him, however, his life went from bad to worse before Our promises were fulfilled.

I understand that it's hard to wait, that hope deferred makes the heart sick (Proverbs 13:12) but I am a God who fulfills My promises. My word will not return to Me void (Isaiah 55:11), therefore, trust in Me and hang onto hope.

You are not here for your own pleasure, you are here for Mine. I delight in you and when I see you walking in continued trust and hope in Me despite your difficult circumstances, I want to scoop you up in My joyful embrace and bless you with even more than you had hoped for or imagined (Matthew 25:21, Ephesians 3:20).

Hang in there, I am proud of you and I love you.

Forever yours,

Jesus

Reflection & Response

The road to promises fulfilled can be like climbing a long and difficult mountain that casts a shadow of despair. It's hard to see the light on the other side when we are stuck in the daily struggle. During the process of hope deferred it can be easy to lose it along the way. I understand because I am walking in it right now with my marriage. God has been showing and promising me something for 8 years. He even gave me a time line and as I come close to the end of that time, I am beginning to tremble in fear wondering if He will come through for me. The temptation to take matters into my own hands or to run away from my promises, hopes, and marriage can be great.

God knows that when He fulfills His promises in my marriage, it will be a tree of life to others, but right now, I feel like giving up because in the flesh it looks hopeless.

What situation looks hopeless to you? _____

_____

God loves giving His children good things (Matthew 7:11) and He is working for our good (Romans 8:28). He fulfills our hearts desires (psalm 37:4) if it lines up with His will and promises (James 4:3). He is *for* relationships and wants us all to enjoy one with Him first and then others (Matthew 22:37-39). He sees that it's not good for man to be alone (Genesis 2:18), and broken marriages is not His mandate (Mark 10:9).

What promises has God been giving you that you have not seen come into fruition yet?

_____

_____

Exercise be creative

Pressing deeper into God is the only way to stay encouraged. Ask Him what He has in mind for you and your life. Read Scripture and devotionals and keep your ears and eyes open to how He speaks to you through people.

Write how God is speaking to you and what He is saying:

_____
_____
_____
_____

Ask Him for what you are wanting and listen to His reply about those things.

_____
_____
_____
_____
_____

Pray with others this week; Jesus encourages this, and He says that our prayers are more powerful in numbers (Matthew 18:20).

she

trusts

without

understanding

proverbs 3:5

Trust in the Lord with all your heart and lean not on your own understanding; in all your ways submit to Him, and He will make your paths straight.

Proverbs 3:5-6

Dear Beautiful One,

There is so much evil, heartache, and confusion in this world and even though I have overcome it (John 16:33) you are still not exempt from experiencing the consequences of sin. Death, disease, and destruction will continue until the day I make all things new and then there will be no more suffering or pain again, and every tear will be wiped away (Revelation 21:4).

Until such time, I am asking you to completely trust Me in all circumstances, even if you don't understand what is happening. I will reveal just enough to keep you going but not too much that you forge ahead without Me.

Don't worry, lay everything before Me and ask Me to take over. I can do this. You don't need to understand everything, you just need to let go and trust Me. I love you.

Forever yours,

Jesus

Reflection & Response

Someone once told me, to compare is to despair. That can be very true but what are your thoughts about the people who are suffering so much while others are living the good life in luxury?_____

Life can be so much harder for some than others and it doesn't seem fair. I don't understand many things but what I do know is that Jesus is compassionate and understands what everyone is going through because He has experienced it all: physical and emotional suffering and abuse, and no one could save Him from it. His purpose was to suffer tremendously. It was His gift to us to go through it on our behalf and that doesn't seem fair either.

Today, Jesus chooses to travel through our pain with us because He says He will always be with us (Matthew 28:20). He has also promised us a helper, the Holy Spirit who will strengthen and guide us through all things (John 14:15-22). He also promises that He will come again and set everything right and there will be justice (Matthew 24). Additionally, If we are desperate (poor in spirit), we can also experience the Kingdom of God (Matthew 5:3) because it is right here (Matthew 3:2). That means really desperate people who run after God will experience His power and presence in this life.

I know God wants to redeem all men to himself and maybe He is giving humanity every chance before He comes again (Titus 2:14). (Read Matthew 24 about the end times).

We can avoid some suffering if we walk closely with Jesus and follow His instructions for our life. It is wise to obey Him, because like any really good parent, He really does have the answers and knows what is good and best for us (Proverbs 19:20, Ephesians 5:15-17). He can ensure we have an amazing life filled with purpose, if we choose to trust Him and listen (Luke 11:28).

Exercise be creative

Look up and read some of the scripture on the previous page .

What stands out to you as being the most interesting and why? _____

_____

_____

_____

_____

_____

_____

_____

Take time to listen to what your Papa God wants you to do this week. It might be just to sing to Him, or rest in Him. Write down what you feel God is saying this week.

_____

_____

_____

_____

_____

_____

_____

She Waits With Expectation

Psalm 5:3

In the morning, Lord, you hear my voice; in the morning I lay my requests before you and wait expectantly.

Psalm 5:3

My Sweet Princess,

I hear and see everything you say and do. I cry (John 11:35) with you and laugh with you. I hold your face in my hands and look into your eyes and tell you everything will be all right (John 14:27).

I want to bless you with good things (Isaiah 30:18) and I am in fact, already working for your good (Romans 8:28). I know it doesn't feel that way sometimes but please trust Me and don't give up hope.

Sometimes waiting for promises to be fulfilled is a fire of endurance that refines you and produces My character within you that will shine like precious gold (Romans 5:3-5). This refining and eventual promises fulfilled will be a testimony of hope for others.

Keep praying, keep waiting, and don't give up. If you endure and persevere, you *will* be rewarded (2 Chronicles 15:7).

Despite the difficulties, failures, and disappointments, always remember that I love you.

Forever yours,

Jesus

Reflection & Response

Have you ever waited for a bus in the freezing cold, or maybe in a long que to get on a roller coaster? The waiting and anticipation can be excruciating. Write down your experiences of waiting for something and how it made you feel?_____

_____

_____

I am a very impatient and somewhat impulsive person. Especially when I am excited or frustrated. Jesus has been telling me to slow down. In 2011, He once showed me a vision of myself in front of a fun park and I was holding His left hand. He said to Me, *"the rides of life can be very exciting, but you must not run ahead, wait with Me and we will go on them together."* We also mused that some rides are scary and some are boring, but no matter what, I am to continue holding His hand.

Four years later, 2015, I had the exact same vision, except this time my husband was holding Jesus' right hand. I said to Jesus: *'it's been four years between the two visions, does that mean it's going to take another four years before I see my prayers answered?'* and I felt in my Sprit Him say: *'yes.'* That would take us up to 2019. Right now, as I write this, it is October 2019 and since 2015, I have been praying, declaring and hoping that a miracle would happen in my husband's life.

So far things have only gotten worse, we have been living separately for the last seven months and we haven't been to church as a family in 5 years. It has been the most difficult, scary, and yet closest journey with Jesus I have experienced so far and it would take a short book to explain all the miracles and stories of how Jesus has been encouraging me along the way. I am declaring restoration in my husband's relationship with Jesus and with me. The waiting right now however, has been harder than ever, but I am being refined all the more for it.

Exercise be creative

It's hard to wait for a promise fulfilled; it's easy to lose hope, especially if you are not being encouraged along the way. I don't know how I would get through my journey without my prayer Warrior Women beside me. If you are facing a battle right now, you need support. If you don't have support, then ask God for a prayer partner or a prayer group that you can be a part of. Come find us on Face-Book *'Warrior Women—fighting for families.'*

This is your exercise this week, to ask God for a prayer partner and start calling each other or face-timing frequently about the situations that you are wanting a break through in.

Write down what this has been like for you.

_____

_____

_____

_____

_____

_____

_____

she is worthy, valuable and recklessly loved

john 3:16

For God so loved the world that He gave His only Son, that whoever believes in Him shall not perish but have eternal life.

John 3:16

Dear Gorgeous One,

I give to you because I love you. I love you because I created you to be exactly who you are. Not the person marked by the sinful world in which you were born, but the real you underneath the hard exterior of self protection and preservation.

If you come to Me just as you are (John 6:37), with your beautiful mess and vulnerability, and honestly share your heart with Me, then I can sew it back together again (Isaiah 61:1, Psalm 147:3).

My death on the cross was the final sacrifice We did for you because you are valuable and because you are worth it. You do not have to *do* anything to gain my love and you are not required to try and be anyone other than yourself (Romans 8:38-39).

I took your shame and your sins. I don't want you to feel burdened by either anymore. If you do wrong, ask for forgiveness and move on immediately, there is no condemnation (Romans 8:1) in Me because I love you unconditionally.

Forever yours,

Jesus

Reflection & Response

When I think about Jesus, I think about abundant life. Life for us mentally, emotionally, and physically. In Him we are free to be ourselves and live the life He has in mind for us, which is always good. Right now we have a spiritual enemy who only wants destruction for us in this life and the next. We have the authority to overcome him though, if we believe the Scriptures. If we don't believe, then we can fall victim to his temptations and deceptions without even knowing it, and that can lead us down a path of self-destruction (John 10:10).

Jesus died for us, so we can freely come and enjoy a relationship with our loving Father. Unconditional love, relationship, acceptance, freedom, the Holy Spirit, and all His spiritual gifts are freely given by Papa God and gift wrapped for us in His son Jesus Christ. We can enjoy this gift that leads to life or reject it. There are natural conse-quences to both choices but free will is our gift also, because He wants a relationship with willing participants.

Have you ever been given a gift by someone that you have never wanted to open? Describe what it is like for you when you first receive a wrapped up gift?

_____

Does the joy and excitement of that gift last a life time?_____

Walking with Jesus is truly a joy, especially when we give Him our 'yes.'

Exercise be creative

This week I encourage you to say, "Yes and Amen," to Jesus. Ask Him what He wants you to do. Ask for confirmation also so that you feel sure you are hearing His voice.

What might He be asking you to do?

_____

_____

_____

Listening and obeying, is like a baby learning to walk. We can stumble over our feet time and again, but the more we practice, the easier it becomes.

Be kind on yourself, it's hard to listen and even harder to obey, but Papa God is there encouraging you every step of the way.

He is our own personal cheer leader.

Blessings to you on your journey as you continue to press into Him.

JENNY MCCONNELL'S TESTIMONY

Spirit of Fire

It was January 1988, a hot summer morning at Avoca Beach in Australia, when my life was radically transformed by an encounter with the Spirit of God.

My parents divorced when I was just seven years old. Ten years later, I was enjoying my annual holiday with my dad and sisters. None of us knew Jesus in a personal way. I was interested in spirituality and owned a deck of tarot cards, but I was not seeking Jesus. To me, church was a dull place for the nerdy Christians in my school, until that fateful morning.

I had never heard of Pentecostals before and I didn't know what speaking in tongues was when a beach mission was handing out flyers to come and join them one evening. I sat watching a film about spiritual warfare. (*For our struggle is not against flesh and blood, but against the rulers, against the authorities, against the powers of this dark world, and against the spiritual forces of evil in the heavenly realms - Ephesians 6:12 NIV*) and after hearing a prayer that spoke to my heart, I accepted their invitation to visit them for a church service the next morning.

I had never experienced a church that sang and worshiped with such enthusiasm. Someone asked me if I would like to receive the gift of tongues. *(For one who speaks in a tongue speaks not to men but to God; for no one understands him, but he utters   mysteries in the Spirit - 1 Corinthians 14:2 ESV.)* I'm the adventurous type, so I thought, why not, and went to the front for prayer.

A few people stood around me and lay hands on me. They asked me to raise my arms in the air and activate my mouth, *"just make a noise,"* they said. So I closed my eyes and said, *"B, B, B, B,"* but nothing was happening, I persisted but still nothing happened. I started feeling self-conscious, and then in my mind, I spoke to God, *"God, if you are really there, now is the time to show up."* (*Ask and it will be given to you—Matthew 7:7 ESV*).

In that moment, a force or energy began in my stomach area, rose up my torso and came out my mouth, and I was uncontrollably yelling out a strange language. At this point, I was unaware of anyone else around me. It was just me and this beautiful, fulfilling Spirit taking over my body, mind and mouth. The only way to describe it was like, swimming in the Spirit.

Time was irrelevant, it felt like ages and yet not long enough before I became aware of the people around me. One of them was saying, "it's okay, bring it down." Slowly, I gained control of my tongue and brought the volume down. When I stopped, I opened my eyes and sobbed. The questions came running. What just happened? Who is this God? What was I experiencing? I wanted to know everything and so I spent the rest of the week learning about Father, Son, and Holy Spirit.

I got baptized in the lagoon, (Acts 2:38) an incredible experience symbolic of burying my sins and my old self and being born again in the spirit with Jesus Christ. I was a new creation (2 Corinthians 5:17), forgiven, righteous, and clean because Jesus became the last atonement for my sins, a sacrificial gift from Father God who paid this price for me (2 Corinthians 5:21). Grace. Mercy. No more striving. He is pleased. It is finished. I don't think anyone in my family quite knew what was happening.

At the same time, however, I also met a boy who lived on the wrong side of the law, but to me he was gorgeous. He was my first boyfriend and a serious distraction. I've learned over the years how Satan is on a mission to work in opposition to what Holy Spirit is doing. He comes to kill, steal, and destroy God's work and our peace, love, joy, families, and lives (John 10:10).

When the holidays ended, my rollercoaster ride began. I was entering grade 12 with such enthusiasm for Jesus, but I was just a newborn learning to walk and it didn't take long before I was dating one boyfriend after another. I had no church or Christian friends to support me *(My people are destroyed from lack of knowledge— Hosea 4:6).* Furthermore, I carried an orphan spirit (a sense of feeling unloved, abandoned, lonely, alienated, and/or isolated—Ephesians 1:5).

Rejection and Insecurities

I struggled with feelings of rejection and insecurities. My father was emotionally and physically distant and my relationship with my mother was codependent and dramatic.

The private school I attended carried a culture of success but I fell through the cracks. I had an undiagnosed hearing impairment and ADHD that left me over-looked and placed in the mystery basket. Year after year throughout high school, I was failing every subject except art. Teachers' concerns, moms' frustrations, and friends' sense of humor created an inner dialogue that started to form my identity. My gift of joy and determination was and is my source of strength, but low self-esteem was their close companion and I was convinced that I was 'dumb.'

Emotional instability instigated my move out of our home at the beginning of university and I lived with students who liked to party. I was stabilized by long-term relationships, but they were fueled with feelings of insecurities and the constant temptation and guilt of sex.

I knew Jesus was with me but there was a gaping hole in my heart and a noise in my head. I was running away from both and into the arms of destruction. I didn't know who I was and I didn't know my worth. My parent's limitations to love and their pain and failures, as well as my own, defined me.

I studied and worked to pay the rent but I almost couldn't complete my degree. Thankfully God blessed me with perseverance and I paid for a tutor to help me through math.

A few years later I went on to do a Masters of Special Education - sensory disabil-ities. Completing this degree was easier as I finally raised the money to get the hearing aids I needed. However, the damage was done and today I still find it difficult to hear, listen, and understand.

Hearing God's Voice

Over the years, however, I have learned to hear *God's* voice. The most obvious time was when I met my husband, David. I was leaving Sydney, Australia, to live in Samoa to teach for a year. Five weeks before leaving, I met David at a mutual friend's farewell. We fell hard and decided to stay together even though we would be miles apart. His plan was to come visit me in six months.

Our time apart was challenging, we were in love but at the same time we had many theological differences. We both believed in Jesus but our similarities seemed to stop there. My experiences growing up, made me feel very anxious about marriage, and I was concerned that this long distance relationship would only end in heartache. Only God knew my future and the best person for me to marry, so it was my intention to find out what He thought.

One night, after a heated debate, on the phone, I took a coin out in desperation and prayed, *"heads, David and I are meant to be together and tails we are not!"* I tossed the coin and it landed on heads. I wasn't satisfied, so I tossed it two more times and both times it landed on heads again. I actually discovered later, that casting lots was a common practice amongst the disciples (Acts 1:26). I still wasn't convinced, however, so I prayed that God would stop David from coming in July if we were not meant to be together. I knew He had the power to do that (Luke 1:37).

When David arrived I was excited to see him and our time together was filled with peace and joy, but the idea of marriage still scared me terribly, so I asked David if we could pray and ask God for an answer. He humored me and so with my little daily bread devotional book, we held hands and I asked God should David and I get married? Then I opened up my devotional to the correct date and in bold letters it said: 'HEADING FOR A WEDDING.'

The answer was clear and three and a half years later we were married. However, neither of us knew exactly how damaged I was until we moved in together.

Come Away with Me

I found being a mother of three boys extremely challenging especially with my eldest having ADHD and the same fiery disposition as me. Additionally, David had retreated emotionally. Resentment smoldered under the surface with occasional but consistent hostile outbursts.

In 2014, I became very disillusioned with being a wife and mother. I felt unloved, rejected, and unappreciated and I felt like giving up. I remember distinctly sitting down and exploring the idea of running away to Italy and grape picking and then I was reminded of a Scripture, *It's no longer I who lives but Christ who lives in me* (Galatians 2:20).

I felt Holy Spirit tug at my heart, "come away with me, spend the first fruits of your time with me."

Inspired by the movie, 'The War Room,' I turned a small storage room in the basement into my prayer room. Each morning I would wake up 45 minutes early to go to this room and read Scripture, listen to worship music, and read devotional books.

Papa God started talking to me in themes. He told me how much He loved me. Our time together was so beautiful, so intimate that I started getting up earlier and earlier. This continued just over a year.

In the same year I met Pastor Gary Meller who worked at a soup kitchen for the homeless. I started volunteering there and listening to him talk about how we are righteous in God's eyes because of Jesus. *God made Him who had no sin to be sin for us, so that in Him we might become the righteousness of God - 2 Corinthians 5:21.*
I learned God does not see my sin because Jesus took it all to the cross for me. That I do not have to earn Papa God's love or strive for it, I can just rest in His arms and receive it and nothing can separate me from it (Romans 8:37-38).

Fears of Abandonment

My fears of abandonment were overwhelming and I sought to control David through all kinds of manipulation as a way to feel safe, secure, and loved. I was jealous, I felt insecure around him, his family, and friends; and I tried to control him and change his choices. My fears and insecurities ran deep and there was nothing I could do to stop them. Today I am grateful for such a strong and steadfast man who persevered with me despite the struggles. *Be kind to one another, tenderhearted, forgiving one another, as God in Christ forgave you - Ephesians 4:32 ESV.*

Moving to Edmonton

In 2006, David was offered a position at the University of Alberta in Edmonton, Canada. We were both unhappy with our careers for different reasons and were excited by the hopes of a new and different life overseas, but it was a huge decision to make. I had to ask God. Within that same week I came across Isaiah 55:12-13 (NIV),

> *You will go out in joy and be led forth in peace; the mountains and hills*
>
> *will burst into song before you, and all the trees of the field will clap their hands.*
>
> *Instead of the thorn bush will grow the pine tree...*

I asked David, "are there pine trees in Edmonton?"

We moved to Canada in January 2007 with a five year plan. When seven years had past, I was becoming quite restless. I longed to go back to family and the ocean but we were happy here too. Life was simple, I didn't have to work full time, I ran a preschool in my basement and worked around having our three children.

Still, I got more and more unsettled about whether we should be staying or going and so I brought my question to the Lord. That very same week, I went to pick up my youngest from his preschool. As I was lining up, I saw another Daily Bread Devotional book, (similar to that in Samoa) and on the front cover were pine trees and the scripture Isaiah 55:12. For me, it was confirmation and my mind was at ease.

I started falling in love with Jesus and His word, declaring it over myself and for my family and my heart started to heal. I began to believe what it said not just with my head but with my heart. *He heals the broken hearted and binds up their wounds - Psalm 147:3 ESV.*

It was in this same year that I decided to paint again. My third boy was in school, so I had the time. I had dabbled in art over the years since high school but nothing significant. My maternal grandmother was an artist and my father became a wonderful artist in his retirement. At first I painted a couple of nudes. Some of my friends asked if I could paint for them as well. I was so encouraged that people wanted to put my art on their walls.

Painting with a Sword

One rainy night we had a prayer group at Pastor Gary and Lori's house. We sat in a circle and he asked us to hold out our hands to receive a gift from God. I distinctly saw in my mind a sword being placed in my hands. A sword is symbolic of the word of God *(Hebrews 4:12)*. I wasn't sure what it meant but I tucked it away in the back of my mind.

I was enjoying my new venture in painting and a couple of months later I stood in front of a blank canvas and said, *"what should I paint now?"* I heard God answer, *"Paint for me."* I was like, of course. My first piece was 'The Cross' based on John 3:16. Ideas started flooding in fast; I had found new purpose and joy as I painted. Later, I realized that my paintbrush had become my sword.

My First Art Walk

In 2016, a friend encouraged me to enter the three day Whyte Avenue Art Walk. I had accumulated about 15 paintings and was ready. A lady named Mariam who runs The Lotus Art Gallery found me on Instagram and invited me to her art walk held on a Sunday one week before the Whyte Ave Art Walk. I saw it as practice and decided to fast for three days *that* weekend in preparation for the big Whyte Avenue event the following weekend.

My First Art Miracle

It seemed like a day of unlikely events. Only one other lady was there to showcase her art and every gallery was closed on that street; furthermore, it was threatening to rain. No one was around. Miraculously, however, as I was setting up, a lady rushed over to me and said that she had to stop and do a U-turn to look more closely at a painting. She couldn't stay but promised she would come back later that day. After she left, it started to rain and we began moving our paintings into the Gallery.

Later in the afternoon, the same lady came back with her father. I write a 'word' with my paintings which she hadn't seen until then. Upon reading this word, she began to cry and felt it spoke directly to her situation. Her father bought the painting for her. It was an incredible experience to sell my first ever painting at $650 and I was on my knees with gratitude after they left.

What really blew me away, however, was when her father returned half an hour later to talk to me. He mentioned how spot on my 'word' was, and asked if I could pray for her. I took his hand and prayed with him right there. When he left, I felt in my spirit God say, "This is what I have called you to do, not just paint my words but to minister my love to people's hearts and minds." *Now to Him who is able to do far more abundantly than all that we ask or think, according to the power at work within us - Ephesians 3:20 ESV.*

Of course the enemy doesn't like us gaining ground for God's Kingdom and I found myself in hospital that same evening with a sty in my eye that left the side of my face swollen and in agony.

Prophetic Artist

The next day I went to PageMaster Publication Services in Edmonton, to pick up some prints of my artwork to sell at the Whyte Avenue Art Walk the following weekend. There, I met Lori Youngman and her husband Dale who owned the company. Lori was showing me around her studio and telling me amazing stories about how her abstract art moves people to tears. How she prays when she paints. She then felt God tell her to show me her latest painting.

When I walked in the room, I saw a magnificent painting. She asked me to sit and said, *"Jenny, what do you see?"* A question she often asks people who are looking at her paintings. I said, *"I see a hand touching fire."* No sooner had the words left my mouth, I began to sob. Holy Spirit had reawaked in me a heart desire to carry the fire of God. I wanted to touch people and see God heal them. She said, *"It is so lovely to meet another prophetic artist."* I hadn't even heard of the term and was still getting my head around people calling me an artist, let alone a prophetic one. It did remind me, however, of a women's conference I attended in 2005 back in Australia. While women were going up to the front to have their head anointed with oil, the lady I went to felt the need to anoint my hands instead. She continued by saying that she could see I will be travelling and that I would be like Deborah in the book of Judges, a prophetess. A word I had tucked away in the back of my mind.

Hearing the Good Shepherd's Voice like a Child

In 2017, my dear friend Cheryl Horn, who is an art therapist, needed to do a project with me for one of her assignments. The assignment was to pick a chapter in the bible, read it, and paint it. Before she came over, my prayer partner Tina, had just randomly text me *John 10:10 -The thief comes only to steal and kill and destroy. I came that they may have life and have it abundantly.* When Cheryl came over she started talking about John 10:10 as well and I exclaimed, *"That's the chapter we have to do."* *John Chapter 10 – The Good Shepherd and His sheep.* The whole chapter is about hearing the voice of God and following it.

I had so much fun painting this Scripture. I was getting small bottles of paint and squeezing them all over the canvas. I felt like a child, giddy with joy and I said, *"This must be what Jesus meant about abundant life!"*

Then I remembered my friend Tina again. About six months earlier she was having tea at my house and God gave her a word for me. It was *'honeysuckle.'* She didn't know what it meant, but it was a childhood memory that I had for-gotten. When I was seven years old, I would sit in the front garden where our honeysuckle tree was and I would pick the flowers off and suck the nectar out. I would do this over and over again. God had used this memory to not only teach me about the joy of living in the moment, like a child, but He was also reminding me to keep my words sweet like honey. *Gracious words are like honeycomb, sweetness to the soul and healing to the body - Proverbs 16:24.*

After that time was over with Cheryl, I was picked up by another friend, Jenny Miller, to go away on a women's retreat. When we had arrived we went to our rooms to drop off our bags. In our room was a card waiting for us. Each year a group of women from another church are given the name of a woman attending the retreat. They pray and ask God for a word of encouragement.

Right at the top of my card was the Bible Verse, *My sheep listen to my voice; I know them, and they follow me - John 10:27.* I squealed with delight. God was speaking to me! Additionally, there was a prophetic artist speaking who gave us an opportunity to hear His voice for someone. It was a treasure hunt exercise and the unique features I heard God give me matched up with the first lady I ap-proached, we were both so excited and I was deeply encouraged by this exercise. I also felt inspired once again to be crossing paths with another prophetic artist.

Randy Clark and Prophetic Art

One week after the women's retreat I heard that Randy Clark was speaking at Gateway Church, Leduc. Randy was a prophet who lived in America and experienced many healings. He wrote a book with Bill Johnson called: *The Essential Guide to Healing.* I started reading this book in 2015, and my faith increased dramatically. In one week, while fasting for the first time, I experienced my first ever miracle of a lady's leg growing out in my hand. Two days after, I experienced a deliverance at my women's prayer group. The following week, at a different prayer group I lay hands on a lady and commanded demons to leave her. She was throwing up foam but set free and God was teaching me about fasting and my authority in Jesus. *Truly, truly, I say to you, whoever believes in me will also do the works that I do; and greater works than these will he do, because I am going to the Father - John 14:12.*

I was transformed by Randy's book, so when Tina told me that Randy was in town in 2017, I had to catch the last day he was going to be there. I was adamant that I was going to receive a word from Randy. After he spoke, he started approaching people who were lining up to receive healing. I could have asked that my hearing be healed but I wanted more than anything for a prophetic word spoken over my life. I had my phone in my hand ready to record and I waited for him to come my way. When he did, I said, *"I just want a word."*

Randy said; *"I believe God wants to use you to give words, I pray there would be a releasing and that you would learn to hear His voice and speak prophetically, that is the word for you, it's what He's going to use you to do. You are going to give words to others and I release the prophetic in your life in the name of Jesus."* Pursue love, and desire the gifts, especially that you may prophecy — 1 Corinthians 14:1. At this point I was undone. It was confirmation number three.

While I was at this service, I picked up their flyer and read that there was a Prophetic Art class coming up. There, I met Angie, a prophetic artist and learned from her about humility before the Lord while painting *(1 Peter 5:6).*

Miracles and Art take Flight

January 2018 was when my art really started taking off. One night I was invited by the River Church to facilitate a 'Paint Night.' This was organised by Cindy Shulz and Melissa Boesch. Around this time Jesus was teaching me the power of declarations. *Truly I tell you, if you have faith as small as a mustard seed, you can say to this mountain, 'Move from here to there,' and it will move. Nothing will be impossible for you— Matthew 17:20.*

I had a gift bag to give to the lucky name that was pulled out of a bucket and before the evening began, Melissa said to me that she never wins anything. My heart went out to her and so I declared right there in front of her that she was going to win the prize tonight in the name of Jesus. I said it with a conviction that even surprised me. About thirty women were there and at the end of the night, Cindy dived her hand into the bucket and pulled out Melissa's name. We screamed with joy and both our faiths were encouraged in that moment.

I was also invited to speak at their women's retreat and guided them in a prophetic painting workshop. I ran prophetic art classes and birthday parties for the young and the old and sold lots of my work. This was the year I also began painting 'My Girls' on 8 x 10" wood boards with paraphrased Scripture down the side. My work was transforming into lyrical art.

Soon after making a few of these girls, my piano teacher suggested that I contact MOSAIC Magazine, since they publish art also. I emailed a few photos and shortly after, the editor contacted me and asked if she could put one of my girls on the front cover and whether I could be a featured artist. I was delighted to be able to share my testimony of God's goodness.

International Justice Mission

Many years ago, God placed in my heart the Scripture that reads; *The kind of fasting I want is this: Remove the chains of oppression and the yoke of injustice, and let the oppressed go free – Isaiah 58:6 - GNT.*

At the beginning of July 2018, I attended a presentation by IJM at Terwillegar Community Church. It was an incredible and heartbreaking movie depicting the life young women endure at the hands of violent and oppressive people. I was clutching the Mosaic Magazine with my girl on the front that I had just picked up and asked; *"what can I do God?"* And the thought came to my mind, *"Give 50% of the profits you make from your 8 x 10" girls to this organization."* It was a strange idea, because I hadn't sold any yet and therefore wouldn't actually be contributing that much.

Art Walks, Separation & Jobs

The Whyte Avenue Art Walk was coming up again and so I decided to make about 15 'girls' and see if they would sell. I was blown away by the response when I added them to my 'Jenny McConnell Artist' Facebook group. They sold quickly for $60 each and I was rapidly making another 15 and then another. I was selling them to people here but also shipping them off to people in America and Australia. I have now sold about seventy and have been contributing 50% of the profits to IJM.

While I was at the Art Walk the Executive Director of 'Art Mentorship Society of Alberta' (AMSA), which is a mental health and wellness program, approached me and asked if I would like to come work for her. This was a dream job come true for me, and I worked there part-time for one year.

December 2019 was the end my nine month 'nesting separation' with my husband. God showed me that I am like a butterfly and my husband is like a tortoise, a vision that holds true to both our personalities and has impacted us both deeply, especially the discovery that butterflies drink tortoise tears. Concurrently, I had spent the last nine months looking for a full-time job, while writing this baby. On 28th February 2020, I received a phone call from 'Chrysalis—An Alberta Society for Citizens with Disabilities' letting me know that I was successfully selected as their art specialist for people with disabilities. I praise God as He continues to bless me in my calling as an artist and an art facilitator.

God is in The Process

Earlier when God was revealing to me that His plan for me was to do art, it took a while before I actually got started. Guilt plagued me, telling me I was not being responsible. Many times I was tempted to get really busy doing work I'm not called to do for the sake of money. I remember distinctly being tempted by three different business ideas in the space of one month; one business model pursued me three times by three different people over two weeks. I remember being on my knees one morning with a heavy heart, praying for direction and I heard a mosquito buzzing in my ear, then I felt it land on my nose so I brushed it away; moments later I opened my eyes and this enormous mosquito was hovering in front of my face. I killed it and I knew the Lord was speaking to me. He was telling me not to be easily distracted by the things of the flesh, what I hear, feel, or see, but to trust Him with all my heart, to not lean on my own understanding but to continue seeking Him and He will make my paths straight (Proverbs 3:5).

God often encouraged me to continue pursuing art. In December 2018, a group of us women organized a Warrior Women's retreat. Cindy Clark facilitated covering a journal with magazine clippings. We would cut pictures out that appealed to us and stick them onto the front and back cover of our journal. It was a beautiful and creative way that God spoke to us personally. There were about 25 women there and about 50 magazines and I picked up the last two magazines that were left. On the front cover of one of the magazines I cut out the words, 'Your True Calling.'

One lady sitting at my table kept finding pictures of brides. I wanted a bride too as it holds so much symbolic meaning of our covenant relationship with Jesus. She offered me one of hers but I declared, as God had taught me, *"I will find one in this magazine, in Jesus name."* Two pages later I not only found a woman in a bridal dress, but she was standing in front of an enormous blank canvas with a paint brush in her hand. We all screamed with astonishment. This was moments before I gave a presentation using my art.

My Hope for You

It is my hope that you would know how much Papa God loves you and who you are in Him. You are unconditionally loved and nothing can separate you from His love. He will never leave you nor forsake you. *Be strong and courageous. Do not fear or be in dread of them, For it is the LORD God who goes with you. He will not leave you or forsake you - Deuteronomy 31:6.*

The Gift and Choice is Yours

Jesus is our LOVE gift from Father God, a gift we can choose to accept or reject. He gave us free will because He desires a relationship with a willing participant. If you choose to accept this gift of LOVE and relationship, it will save you in ways you never dreamed possible. This salvation is for your mind, body, and soul in this life and the next. Jesus paid the highest price He could, to give you this gift. A gift of Grace and Mercy that can never be earned.

Ask Him to forgive you in every detail you feel you need forgiveness. Sit quietly with Him and ask Him to remind you of what you need to repent of. He will graciously forgive you for everything, if you ask. He never condemns, He will only gently move us towards repenting and asking for forgiveness. This is called feeling convicted. The enemy, however, will want you to ruminate and oppress you with the burden of guilt and shame. This is called condemnation, so be aware of the difference. Asking for forgiveness can sometimes be a daily occurrence as we get to know Him. He will gently push, guide and refine us. This is a life time journey of growing from Glory to Glory in Him (2 Corinthians 3:18).

Your choice to accept Jesus as your; brother, lover and friend automatically qualifies you to be adopted into His family and Heavenly Kingdom , *But to all who did receive him, believed in his name, gave the right become children of God - John 1:12.*

You would be a co-heir ... *and if children, then—heirs of God and fellow heirs with Christ, we suffer with him in order that we may also be glorified with him (Romans 8:17)*, and co-laborer with Jesus ...*For we are fellow workers (1 Corinthians 3:9, seated in heavenly places with Him... and raised us up with him and seated us with him in the heavenly places in Christ Jesus (Ephesians 2:6).*

You would be a princess, a queen, and royalty, given all authority to overcome Satan, darkness and demons as well as sickness and disease...*Behold, I have given you authority tread on serpents and scorpions, and over all the power of enemy, and nothing shall hurt you - Luke 10:19.* You would be more than a conqueror in Jesus (Romans 8:31-39) and have access to an intimate, loving relationship with Him .(*You are altogether beautiful my darling, beautiful in every way—Song of Songs 4:7).*

This is His heart for you....

Please pray:

Father God in Heaven, please forgive me for going my own way, I want to go your way and have a loving relationship with you. I also forgive... (name people you need to forgive, who have hurt you).

Jesus, I accept you as my Lord and Savior, thank you for washing me clean and making me righteous by your blood.

Holy Spirit I invite you into my heart and my life, please guide me and teach me how to listen to the voice of Papa God and obey.

If you prayed this prayer with your heart, then I encourage you to get plugged into a church. Ask God which one and see what happens, go with *His* flow. When you get there, talk about being baptized. It is important to find a family of believers, because the enemy wants to rob you of this new life you are about to embark on. He will come full force at you and do whatever he can to prevent you joining. He will use; offense, rejection, alienation, and temptation, so be on the look out and tell him to go away in the name of Jesus, you have that authority now.

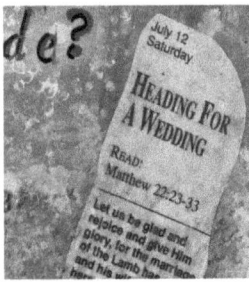

1997: I really wanted God to tell David and I if we should get married or not. We held hands and prayed and then I opened my Daily Bread Devotional and it said: 'HEADING FOR A WEDDING.'

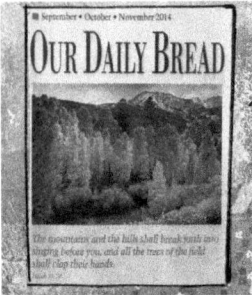

2007: I was seeking God's guidance as to whether we should accept David's job offer in Edmonton. I came across Isaiah 55:12-13, *'instead of the thorn bush would be the pine trees.'*

2014: I was feeling very restless and asked God if He wanted us to stay in Edmonton?—God gave me the same scripture - Isaiah 55:12. It was on the front cover of the Daily Bread, when picking up my son Ewan at pre-school, days after praying and asking God for guidance.

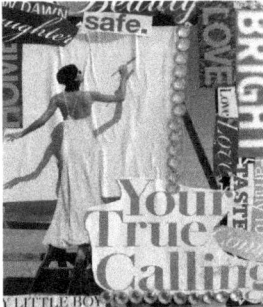

December 2018: I declared that I would come across a bride in my magazine. I find one in front of a canvas with a paint brush in her hand. God confirms again that He is calling me to be an artist. To paint for Him.

December 2019: I received a vision that David is like a tortoise and I am like a butterfly. That he stabilizers me and I bring him lightness and joy. Interesting that I actually have low blood pressure and butterflies need the sodium from tortoise tears.

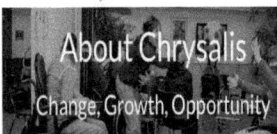

February 2020: I received a phone call from 'Chrysalis' letting me know I have the full time position as an art facilitator.

Identity Declaration

I am victorious in life. I am more than a conqueror (Romans 8:31). I am an overcomer because of Christ Jesus in me (John 16:33).

THIS IS MY IDENTITY

The favor of God surrounds me like a shield (Psalm 5:12). I have favor in the sight of all men (Proverbs 3:4). God goes before me making the crooked places straight (Isaiah 45:2), and opening doors that no man can shut (Revelation 3:8).

THIS IS MY IDENTITY

I have the mind of Christ and hold the thoughts, feelings, and purposes of His heart (1 Cor. 2:16). I have the mind of the Holy Spirit which is life and peace. I am living the life of the Spirit (Galatians 5:25). The Holy Spirit dwells within me and directs me (Romans 8:9).

THIS IS MY IDENTITY

I am anointed by the Holy Spirit and I know the truth (1 John 2:20). The Holy Spirit is leading me and guiding me into all truth (John 16:13). He is revealing hidden things to me (Jeremiah 33:3).

THIS IS MY IDENTITY

I have been born again of the incorruptible seed of the Word of God which lives and abides forever (1 Peter 1:23). I am a new creation in Christ. Old things have passed away and all things have become new (2 Corinthians 5:17). I am created in the image of God and in His likeness (Genesis 1:27). I am seated with Christ in heavenly places (Ephesians 2:6).

THIS IS MY IDENTITY

I am the righteousness of God in Christ Jesus (2 Corinthians 5:21). I am in right standing with God (Romans 1:17). I am accepted in the beloved (Ephesians 1:5-6). God loves me and nothing can separate me from His love (Romans 8:31). I am sanctified, consecrated, and separated from the world (John 15:19). I am a child of God (1 John 3:1), and I am one with God (John 14:20).

THIS IS MY IDENTITY

I am strong in the Lord and in the power of His might (Ephesians 6:10). I am empowered through my union with Him (Philippians 4:13). I am anointed (1 John 2:20).

THIS IS MY IDENTITY

I have been created by God to prosper and make a difference in this world (Jeremiah 29:11). I am a success. I am the head. I am above (Deuteronomy 28:13). I am blessed (Jeremiah 17:7-8).

THIS IS MY IDENTITY

I am redeemed from sickness and disease (Mark 5:34). Sickness, disease, viruses ,and infections cannot live in my body (Psalm 41:3). My body is the temple of the Holy Spirit (1 Corinthians 6:19). The law of the Spirit of life in Christ Jesus flows throughout every cell, organ, and tissue of my body. By His stripes I am healed (Isaiah 53:5).

THIS IS MY IDENTITY

I am free from fear and anxiety. I fear not, for God is with me (Isaiah 41:10). I do not fret or have anxiety about anything. I do not have a care. I think on what is good, lovely, and worthy of praise (Philippians 4:8). I believe in Jesus and I will never be disappointed or put to shame (Romans 10:11). I let the peace of God rule in my heart, deciding and settling with finality all questions that arise in my mind (Colossians 3:15).

THIS IS MY IDENTITY

I am being transformed by the renewing of my mind Romans 12:2). I let the Word of God dwell in me richly (Colossians 3:16). I am meditating in the Word day and night, making my way prosperous and dealing wisely in all the affairs of my life (Joshua 1:8).

THIS IS MY IDENTITY

The Lord is my Shepherd and I am not in want (Psalm 23:1). My God supplies all my needs according to His riches in glory by Christ Jesus (Philippians 4:19). I am a tither and the windows of heaven are open over my life. The blessings of the Lord are overtaking me (Malachi 3:10).

THIS IS MY IDENTITY

No weapon formed against me shall prosper (Isaiah 54:17). I tread upon serpents and scorpions and over all the works of the enemy and nothing shall hurt me (Luke 10:19). I lay hands on the sick and they recover (Mark 16:17). I cast out demons in Jesus' name (Matthew 10:8). I take my shield of faith and I quench every fiery dart of the wicked one (Ephesians 6:16). Greater is He Who is in me than he who is in the world (1 John 4:4).

THIS IS MY IDENTITY

I am royalty, chosen, and loved (1 Peter 2:9). I can do all things through Christ which strengthens me (Philippians 4:13). I have marvelous gifts that God has placed within me to be a blessing for others (1 Peter 4:10). I am blessed and enriched abundantly. All my needs are met so that I can be a blessing and sow into the lives of others (2 Corinthians 8-9).

THIS IS MY IDENTITY

Jenny McConnell was born and raised in Sydney, Australia. She moved to Canada in 2007 with her husband where they raised their three boys.

Jenny has a Masters in Special Education and an Associate Diploma in Creative Arts.

Jenny continues to facilitate art groups and sell her artwork.

www.jennymcconnellartist.com